A Week from Next Tuesday

A Week from Next Tuesday

Joy Keeps Showing Up
(Because Christ Keeps Showing Up)

Matthew A. Rich

Foreword by
Thomas W. Currie III

WIPF & STOCK · Eugene, Oregon

A WEEK FROM NEXT TUESDAY
Joy Keeps Showing Up (Because Christ Keeps Showing Up)

Wipf & Stock
An Imprint of Wipf and Stock Publishers
199 W. 8th Ave., Suite 3
Eugene, OR 97401
www.wipfandstock.com

ISBN 13: 978-1-62032-299-4
Manufactured in the U.S.A.

To Sarah
Who always helps me see more clearly

Contents

Foreword

THERE ARE TWO THREATS that any theologian faces when attempting to interpret what the gospel means by joy. The first is that he or she will make this fruit of the Spirit seem easy and sweet, as if the Christian life were characterized by one upbeat moment after another. This is a real temptation because Scripture knows of such "mountaintop moments" and affirms as its central witness the triumph of Jesus Christ over the darkness of sin and death. Who could not be joyous in the face of such good news? We should not be surprised, though inevitably we are, at how often the New Testament writers themselves seem to go overboard. Their joy raises the question: does the victory of Easter mean the end of history (Acts 1:6), or does the superabundance of God's grace mean that we may now sin at leisure (Rom 6:2), or does the sustaining strength of the church's witness mean that we can finesse the cost of our own witness (Heb 12)? The problem Christians face, these texts suggest, is not the poverty of grace but its abundance, not the timidity of Spirit but its fullness, not the lack of joy but its exuberance. So, it would be easy to conclude that joy in the Christian life is easy, a kind of "positive attitude" that every disciple needs to cultivate and practice. Our happy-face culture understands this attitudinal virtue and is more than ready to hear the gospel in such terms and even contrive formulas that will make that kind of joy happen.

But what the gospel means by joy is not that at all. Rather, it is a gift. Joy is the "fallout," the radiation left in the world by the resurrection of Jesus Christ from the dead. It is neither something we can contrive nor something we can manufacture, and it comes to us wrapped not in the saccharine folds of our own agendas but in the grave cloths neatly folded in an empty tomb. Those cloths held a dead man, one who was crucified and whose cross has become the unwanted and even scandalous sign of his victory. That cross is what helps us resist trivializing joy into something we find merely sweet, just as the cross is what describes the labor that brings real joy into the world. Joy comes in no other way, which is why the temptation to sweeten it into something more marketable and less mysterious must always be resisted.

The second temptation, however, is worse, and that is to conclude that the gospel is devoid of joy, a grim work of moral self-improvement or precise social justice that reduces the grace of our Lord Jesus Christ to the "measurable objectives" of what we deem sufficient. Sadly, it is very easy to succumb to this temptation and miss the gospel's deep joy while we busy ourselves with supposedly more important matters. Elder brothers, new and old Pharisees, competing disciples, and virtuous rich young rulers of every age habitually take this route and soon starve to death on their own sufficiency. The invitation they and we so often find baffling is the invitation to joy. Can you come to the banquet? Can you "rejoice with me" that the lost sheep or lost coin or lost son has been found? Can you embrace the joy the waiting Father insists on giving you?

Matt Rich has heard these questions, and in this marvelous book has enabled the rest of us to see the gift of joy that is at the heart of the gospel. In so doing, he has resisted both the temptation to trivialize this gift into something more formulaic and the temptation to reduce the gospel to a joyless enterprise of moral or social self-improvement. All of which makes this book itself a real gift: not a strategy, not a manual of instruction, not a list of things to do, but a gift that seeks to feed our hearts and souls. To write such a book is not a timid undertaking but represents something bold. This book is ambitious; it seeks to inspire and, yes, transform, your life. Only a gift of the Spirit can do such a thing. Precisely because what Matt has presented here is so unformulaic it can speak of the fruit of the Spirit as true joy and invite you and me to rejoice with him in the gift that the Spirit makes possible in Jesus Christ. We all need joy. Indeed, we need this gift more than we care to admit. But even more, the church's witness is in need of the joy of its own message. This book serves the church well in reminding us of the gift of joy that Christ insists on giving to those who seek to follow him.

As the Prayer book says, I would invite you to "read, mark, learn, and inwardly digest" what this book has to say. In doing so, you will find great joy.

—Thomas W. Currie III
Charlotte, NC

Acknowledgments

ACCORDING TO THE FOURTEENTH century theologian Master Eckhart, "If the only prayer you ever say in your entire life is 'thank you,' it will be enough."[1] I pray those two words are enough as I come to the end of this project, because I can only express my gratitude to the many who have provided great assistance along the way.

Pastoral and writing mentors Martin Copenhaver and Lillian Daniel selected me as one of twelve aspiring "Working Pastors, Writing Pastors" to join them at the Collegeville Institute in Collegeville, Minnesota, for a week during the summer of 2011 to talk, pray, dream, and write. In the year and a half since that seminar, Martin and Lillian have both patiently answered my endless emails and encouraged me along the way.

I owe a great debt to my colleagues in that writing seminar as well. As I shared with them a brief outline of my doctor of ministry work on "Christian Joy, Young Adults, and Sabbath Practices," time and time again they said, "I would really like to read more about that." Upon finishing my degree, I put my thesis on the shelf to gather dust and chose to focus my efforts on catching up on sleep and pastoring a growing congregation. Yet, the Holy Spirit tugged at me each time a colleague expressed interest in reading more about joy. Much to my own surprise, I returned from that week in Minnesota with a draft of a book proposal, which I then began sending off to publishers.

I have rarely felt the combination of elation and fear I experienced when, in the middle of a family dinner, the e-mail from editor Christian Amondson at Wipf & Stock arrived. I thank Christian,

1. Muller, *Sabbath*, 128

Mike van Mantgem, and everyone at Wipf & Stock for their help in turning an idea from a vague proposal into the work before you today.

My family, friends, and colleagues Brian Blount, Tom Currie, Christopher and Colleen Edmonston, Katie Gottlieb, Jack Haberer, Heidi Haverkamp, Matt Nichol, and Kristie and Chad Rush have all read parts, if not all, of this book and offered their suggestions. They pushed me to be more precise, to tell more stories, and to share my own struggles to know joy. Their words of grace and truth greatly improved this book. I share a special word of gratitude to Tom Currie, a mentor and friend, who first introduced me to the wonders of Christian joy through an early draft of his own work. Through the years he has carefully helped me read, write, and preach of the joy that is rightfully ours in Christ. That Tom would agree to write the Foreword to this book is a true gift.

For the last six years God has blessed me with the opportunity to serve as pastor of First Presbyterian Church, Lumberton, North Carolina. The saints of Lumberton have supported me in my initial efforts to write, and they have listened to their fair share of sermons on joy. In more ways than I can count, we see Christ together and know joy. I must say a particular word of gratitude to the young adults of the Bread for the Journey Sunday School class who began a journey toward knowing Sabbath and joy several years ago, to the Wednesday Morning Men's Bible Study who reflected upon the Scriptures studied within this book as it neared completion, and to Charlotte Nye and Dolli Adams who asked me about once a month when I am going to write a book. I pray they find a glimpse of the gospel in these pages.

And finally to my family. In the midst of the busyness that marks our lives, the tragedy and suffering that surround us, and the burdens we carry, we glimpse Christ and know joy. As much as this book contains my stories of looking for joy, it is also full of our stories together: Will's science fair project and piano lessons, Sam's baseball team and boundless energy, Bekah's rocking out on her bed and her hand in mine as we celebrate communion. My wife Sarah's wisdom about the joy of the gospel, and her ability to keep our lives somewhat sane, far surpasses my own. God blessed me with a true partner with which to walk through this life and with whom to know love and look for joy. My parents, Doug and Cookie Rich, and my mother-in-law, Nancy Terry, have provided unwavering support to both Sarah and me throughout this project. For all of them, my heart overflows with gratitude.

The quest continues. We never know where or when Christ might show up next. Yet for a moment, I pause once more to say simply, "thank you."

To God be the Glory!

—Matthew A. Rich
Lumberton, NC
All Saints Day, 2012

Introduction

Something More

DRIVING DOWN A MOUNTAIN road somewhere between western North Carolina and eastern Tennessee, my wife Sarah and I were in the car alone. No, we had not left our kids crying at the last rest stop, the air filled with squealing tires and dust. This was the one weekend we attempt to take every year just for us. In truth, the kids barely missed us amid the flurry of activity with their grandparents. We were on the road.

It was fall. The leaves on the trees created a kaleidoscope of color. Oranges, reds, and yellows all mixed with the deep greens of tall pines. Around every bend the colors shifted and changed. Clear Carolina blue colored the sky. No other cars on the road. The mountains of Tennessee beckoned. Just the two of us. About as good as it gets.

This was still in the days, about eight years ago, when people listened to CDs. Maybe you, like me, still listen to CDs, but I fear our days are numbered. Sarah hit eject on the car's CD player, removed the disk of practically worn out VeggieTales' "Backyard" songs, and put in another CD. We smiled as the guitar chords of a familiar song began. A new band in country music, Sugarland, had just released their second big hit. Drumming to the beat on the steering wheel and dash, joining our voices with the distinct twang of the female lead singer, we sang along about the struggles of waking up on Monday morning, filling a coffee cup on the way out the door, enduring highways that stood still with traffic, and barely making it to work on time. I remember thinking to myself,

"How often does my morning begin with exactly that kind of hurried pace, fueled by coffee and the anxiety of always being late? And I only live two blocks from the church!"

The lyrics flowed seamlessly into the chorus as we continued to sing along about how there has to be "something more" than the hurried pace, hard times, and burdens of daily life. In the brief interlude before the next verse began, Sarah looked at me and said, "That's it, isn't it? That's what we're all looking for—something more." And I knew that she was right.

The weekend ahead would be a mountaintop experience. A quaint log cabin in the hills. No alarm clock in the morning. Leisurely meals at nice restaurants. A pause from the pressing realities of daily life. A break from the busyness, the tragedy, and the rat race. The weekend was a trip away—a chance to find a little less hard time and a little more bliss. Some might even call it "joy." But come Sunday afternoon, we headed back down the mountain, back to real life. Was it possible to know the bliss of the mountain when we returned? What about a week from next Tuesday when we reached the plains, or even the valleys, of our everyday world?

At the time of our weekend getaway, I had just started putting together ideas for what would become my doctor of ministry project on Christian joy and young adults. I knew that Jesus told his disciples that their "joy shall be complete" (John 15:11). The apostle Paul even commands the church in Philippi to "rejoice in the Lord always" (Phil 4:4)! And yet, it seemed that so many people in the church lacked joy.

A few friends and I had started posing questions about joy as we planned for a church retreat. Questions like:

- What is joy?
- How do you rejoice when there is so much to do?
- How can you be joyful when your two-year-old seems possessed?
- How do you rejoice when your project is due at work and the computer crashes?

- How can you be joyful when the evening news keeps you up at night?

- How do you find joy amid the increasing demands of work, family, and church?

Even for young adults like Sarah and me, committed to the church and engaged in wonderful and faithful ministry, Christian joy often seemed elusive at best. So on a beautiful day, on a mountain road, with the kids at home with the grandparents, we sang together, "There's got to be something more."

This book is the result of several years of my own searching for and writing about the something more that Christians call "joy." What I have discovered is that joy is not something we find, create, achieve, or produce. Joy is messy. It is not easy to define nor is it simply a feeling or an emotion. While I pray you will know joy after reading this book, I can promise you that these pages do not contain a three step plan to have more joy in your life. After reading that last sentence you may be tempted to put down this book, find my telephone number on the Internet, and call me to demand your money back. However, I ask you to abide just a little longer in these pages, because I hope that you will discover what I now know:

Joy is a gift received
when we know Christ's presence with us.

I can assure you that my journey to know joy has not always been easy. Indeed, my journey is ongoing; I myself am still looking for complete joy. Let me put it this way: The questions my friends and I posed about joy in preparation for that retreat were not theoretical. These are still the questions that I have about joy in my own life. At the time of that weekend retreat, I served as pastor of a two-hundred-member congregation. I thought I was busy with preaching, leading worship, working with committees, and visiting members at the hospital and in their homes. Sarah worked four days a week as an attorney for a large law firm. Our boys, Will and Sam, were four and two. They kept us occupied, mostly because they would destroy any room if we left them alone for too long. I often felt like I had too much to do, that my two-year-old was possessed, that my old computer crashed every time I started working on a sermon, and that I could not watch the evening news because I worried about a friend who was serving as an Army chaplain in Iraq. I chose the topic of joy for my project because I was looking for joy.

Fast-forward to today. I now serve as pastor of a 550 member congregation. I think I am busy with preaching, leading worship, working with committees, supervising church and preschool staff, and visiting members at the hospital and in their homes. I serve on a city commission for community relations, regional church committees, and advisory boards for a seminary and a denominational magazine. Sarah works from home for a large bank on projects that provide her flexibility with her time but also can demand great attention at key moments. She serves as a board member of the PTA and devotes time to the board of a community early childhood education and development agency. Our boys, now ten and eight, have been joined by a sister, Bekah, who is five. They keep us occupied constantly. They manage to destroy their bedrooms if we leave them alone for too long. However, reading stories, coaching soccer, coaching baseball, leading Cub Scout dens, and driving to ballet and piano lessons occupies most of my time with the kids. While not long ago Sarah and I complained that we had an event or activity every night of the week, this past year we found ourselves trying to get the kids to two or three activities every night of the week. Sarah and I both have cousins who are receiving treatment for cancer. Plus I am now also writing a book about Christian joy.

While I would not change a moment of the life I lead, I always feel like I have too much to do. All three of my children occasionally attempt to drive me crazy. The only time I can get on the computer at home is after midnight. I learn about the world by watching late night comedy shows, because that is the only way I can keep up with current events without tears. As my journey continues there are occasional mountaintop moments, but most of my life is spent in the plains and the valleys. Yes, ordinary days today, tomorrow, and a week from next Tuesday.

Maybe your life looks and feels at least a little like mine.

And yet, I want you to know that in the midst of the busyness, tragedy, and burdens of life, you and I still might know joy. In this book I hope to give you a glimpse of that amazing gift so that you might begin to see it in your own life. For joy is a gift, an essential mark of Christian discipleship, that cannot be lost or stolen. When we see Christ, no matter what the circumstances in which we find ourselves, we will know joy.

If you are still ready to put the book down, call me up, and demand your money back, then now is the time to do so. I look forward to hearing from you. But if you find that you too are looking for something more than you have been able to create for yourself, for something that just might be a gift, for something that promises to sustain you in the busy and often tragic life you live, then I invite you to turn the page. For it is not just on the mountaintop, but in the midst of life today, tomorrow, and a week from next Tuesday, that Christ is with us. Yes, Christ is with you and with me. And when Christ is present and we notice him, there is joy.

Questions for Reflection

1. Think about a "mountaintop" experience in your own life, not related to your church or faith. What made it such a great experience?

2. Describe a time in your life when you have known what you would call "joy." What made that moment a gift?

3. What do you most hope to discover through reading this book?

1

Rejoice in the Lord

Philippians 4:4–7 and John 15:1–11

WHAT DO YOU EXPECT to hear when reading a letter from prison? If you open your Bible to the book of Philippians, you will find one prisoner's tale. The most powerful empire of his day held him captive under house arrest. His ability to spread the gospel by traveling to new towns and places, gone. His hope of reaching Spain to found churches there, dashed. Under the watchful eyes of his captors, he writes to a fledgling church in Philippi, a church that is itself under threat of persecution. During his imprisonment he watched as the one man who would carry this letter to this beloved church suffered through a devastating illness that nearly took his life. There was great cause for despair.

Nevertheless, in the midst of such circumstances, the apostle Paul exclaims:

> Rejoice in the Lord always; again I will say, Rejoice! Let your gentleness be known to everyone. The Lord is near. Do not worry about anything, but in everything by prayer and supplication with thanksgiving let your requests be made known to God. And the peace of God which surpasses all understanding will guard your hearts and your minds in Christ Jesus (Phil 4:4–7).

Rejoice? Always? In those circumstances? No wonder Paul had to say it twice. In light of his circumstances, he cannot be serious. And yet he is.

An Endless Pursuit

Paul's words about joy, while he is in prison, seem odd to our modern sensibilities. This is because we often describe joy as being an emotion akin to happiness and/or pleasure. When asked, "What do you hope for your children when they grow up?" most parents respond, "That he or she will be happy." Happiness has become life's goal. That is, the chief end of humanity is to feel happiness and pleasure at all times. We teach our children that if they are happy and they know it, they should clap their hands, stomp their feet, and shout "Amen!" Now I love that song, but I am still working on how to do all three of those things at the same time. However, it seems that today's parents expect, and often intervene to ensure, a lot of clapping, stomping, and Amens from their children!

As much fun as it is to clap, stomp, and shout "Amen," it seems to me that we are teaching our children the wrong message. For the pursuit of happiness is a foolish goal. But why? To discover the answer, we must first understand the true nature of happiness. So, what is happiness?

Happiness is an emotional response and pleasure is a physical response, but both depend on external circumstances. If our external circumstances are pleasant—for example, our basic needs are met and we have the approval of our friends—then we generally feel happy with our lives. If we graduate from a good college, have a "cool" job, if we are able to travel, live in a nice home, buy nice things, and even have the material wealth to show compassion to others, then we have the external requisites for the emotion of happiness.

Our emotional happiness can also depend upon another important external factor—getting what we think we have earned or deserve. We expect others to reward us for our hard work, and when they do, our expectations are met and we feel happy. However, when we work extremely hard, when we complete a task or assignment above our own expectations, but our boss, our friends, or our family fails to recognize our achievements, then our expectations are not met and we are unhappy.

The emotion of pleasure works in much the same way. If our physical needs are met—if we are not hungry, thirsty, hot, cold, exhausted, or in pain—then we experience pleasure. Even if we do have some pain, or have lost some functions of our body, we can often take enough medicine to mask those ills, and so know pleasure. Yet, the moment the medicine wears off, when we step out of the air-conditioned room on a hot summer day, when our stomach growls and we stand before an empty refrigerator—our pleasure disappears.

Think about your own life for a minute. Think about the things that make you happy and/or bring you pleasure. Maybe your thoughts drift to the moments when you are with your family for the holidays. The house is full and everyone there makes you happy. Yet at some point, children grow up, move out, and establish homes of their own. The holiday ends and everyone has to go back to work. The house is empty again. While we achieve happiness for a moment, we cannot sustain it.

Every temporal happiness and pleasure works in that way. It makes you happy to cook, but you cannot cook twenty-four hours a day, 365 days a year.

It makes you happy to eat. You push yourself back from the table after enjoying a gourmet dinner; you are full of pleasure. However, it is not but a few hours later that you are hungry again.

It makes you happy to read, and you become immersed in a book. But the book ends and as it does, so does your happiness.

You are playing golf, and for the first time in your life you hit a hole in one! You are happy beyond words! But then your next drive hooks off into the woods, and you realize there are fourteen more holes left to play.

You root for a college basketball team. They do well, maybe even win the national championship. However, as soon as the season ends, you realize that there is a season next year. Winning one championship is no longer good enough. Your team needs to win every year in order for you to be happy.

Do you see that when happiness becomes the goal, it almost ensures we will never actually be happy? While the pursuit of happiness has been engrained into the American ethos, so often that quest leads to despair instead of joy; to an emptiness and lack of purpose; to boredom and an endless quest for novelty. Happiness as a byproduct of a well-lived life is wonderful, but happiness as a goal is ultimately an unachievable standard. The endless pursuit of happiness paradoxically prevents Christians from knowing Paul's joy.

Rejoice in the Lord

What does Paul mean when he says "Rejoice always!" if he is not talking about happiness and pleasure? We might turn first to Paul's letter to the Galatians. In the fifth chapter of Galatians, Paul commands his readers to, "Live by the Spirit and do not gratify the desires of the flesh" (Gal 5:16). He goes on to provide a list of vices that accompany the desires of the flesh. In contrast to this vile way of life, Paul commends to the Galatians the "fruit of the Spirit: love, joy, peace, patience, kindness, generosity, faithfulness, gentleness, and self-control" (Gal 5:22–23). As you can see, joy makes the list at number two.

Due to its prominent mention as a characteristic fruit of the Spirit, explorations of Christian joy often go no further. Whether joy is an emotion or a feeling does not really matter because it is a byproduct of the Holy Spirit. Joy is connected to the Holy Spirit.

Many of the Christians I know are somewhat uncomfortable with the Holy Spirit. God the Father who created everything—we are good with that. God the Son, Jesus, who gave his life for us—we have a handle on that, too. But God the Holy Spirit, an elusive entity to whom we cannot ascribe human traits, makes us a bit nervous. So if joy is indeed a characteristic fruit of the Spirit, perhaps it is natural for many us to stop right there—even though joy makes the list just behind love. After all, joy cannot really be distinguished from all the rest of the fruits of the Spirit, right? These Christians will just enjoy a Spirit-filled fruit salad in which joy adds a little flavor but gets lost between love and peace.

Instead of giving up on the mysteries of joy, let us instead return to the text with which we began this chapter. Paul writes quite clearly in his letter to the Philippians. He does not urge the Philippians to be happy or to lighten up and have some fun. He does not mention the Holy Spirit here. Instead, Paul practically commands the church in Philippi to "Rejoice *in the Lord* always; again I say Rejoice . . . *the Lord is near*" (Phil 4:4). I added the emphasis to these verses so that you did not miss the key for Paul's understanding of joy. Joy is not an emotion that comes and goes depending on our circumstances. Joy is a characteristic fruit of the Spirit, but not one to be lost in a fruit salad. No, joy is a reality that may be known—a gift known in the real presence of Jesus Christ. It would be absurd for Paul to command anyone to rejoice if the circumstances of imprisonment and potential persecution provide the only reason to do so. Instead, to invite others to rejoice because *the Lord is near* is to offer a wondrous gift.

Orthodox priest and theologian Alexander Schmemann describes the connection between joy and the presence of Christ when he writes, "A Christian is one who, wherever he looks, finds Christ and rejoices in Him. And this joy transforms all his human plans and programs, decisions and actions, making all his mission the sacrament of the world's return to Him who is the life of the world."[1] Not dependent upon physical circumstances, mood, or feeling, joy is an encounter with Christ. Joy is a gift known when we see the risen Christ who is Emmanuel—God with us "always, even to the end of the age" (Matt 28:20).

"Knowing" Joy

Christian joy is a gift *known in Christ's presence.* Notice that I did not say Christians "feel" joy in Christ's presence. Feelings are fickle. We can manipulate feelings easily. Feelings come and go depending upon circumstances. However, joy has an objective reality that may

1. Schmemann, *For the Life*, 113.

be known. Joy is a gift received. It is Christ's gift to you. So, as you know Christ, you might know joy.

Knowledge sometimes gets a bad reputation in the church because we have ceded that term to the realm of science. In our world today, if you want to "know" something, you have to be able to prove it. The scientific method proscribes the steps needed to obtain knowledge. Simply follow those steps and you can take a hypothesis and turn it into a fact. For example, I once helped my son Will with a science fair project for school. He wanted to "know" which would fly the farthest when launched from his homemade catapult: a small marble, a cotton ball, a marshmallow, or a Hershey's Kiss. He thought it would be the marble because it weighed the most.

Therefore, to test his theory, together we constructed an experiment. We first weighed each of the objects. We discovered that indeed the marble did weigh the most. The cotton ball and the marshmallow were equally light, with the Hershey's Kiss in the middle.

Then we tested Will's hypothesis. After repeatedly launching the four objects down the hallway in our house and then carefully measuring the distance flown by each, the marshmallow clearly flew the farthest. The marble was not even close. With a little more research, we determined that the marshmallow flew farther than the marble due to its lighter weight, and it outdistanced the cotton ball due to its more aerodynamic shape. Therefore, based on our scientific experiment and rational evaluation of the data, we now had "knowledge." We could finally eat the Hershey's Kiss and marshmallow, too.

However, to "know" joy is not just to make a connection in one's brain. To know joy is not just to have memorized the correct facts about Christ or to have conducted an experiment with prayer. Knowing joy is not even to have read this book (as much as I pray you find joy within these pages). No, to "know" joy is to perceive Christ's presence, and not just with the mind but also with the heart.

Knowing joy in this way is akin to how the Protestant reformer John Calvin described faith as being "a firm and certain knowledge of God's benevolence toward us founded upon the truth of the freely given promise in Christ both revealed to our minds and sealed upon our hearts through the Holy Spirit."[2] Thus, to know joy combines the perception of truth with our minds and the presence of Christ planted deep within our hearts.

Perhaps we can think of knowing joy in this way. Again, let me tell you about my son, Will. When not launching objects down the hallway of our house, Will is learning to the play the piano. We are quite proud of him as he has quickly taken to this instrument. To nurture his gift, and to ensure that practice is more enjoyable than it is drudgery, we bought Will the sheet music from one of his favorite movies: *Star Wars*. The first piece he picked to play was "Imperial March," the theme song for Darth Vader. If you have ever seen this movie, you may have read that last sentence and immediately began humming the distinct and foreboding tune that always accompanies Vader when he enters a room. So to "know" Darth Vader is not just to recognize him with our minds when we see him in his black helmet, suit, and cape. To know Darth Vader is also to hear that music and not just feel, but know in your heart, that the villain has arrived.

What if joy is Christ's theme song? What if joy is a gift that allows us to know when we recognize Christ with our minds and hear his song in our hearts?

The American Puritan preacher and theologian Jonathan Edwards knew joy as being the presence of Christ in his mind and heart. It may surprise you to hear me mention Jonathan Edwards in a book about Christian joy because many people know Edwards from a single sermon: "Sinners in the Hands of an Angry God." This sermon, preached by Edwards in an attempt to awaken a particularly hard-hearted congregation, rails against human sin and warns of God's unquenchable wrath for those who do not repent.

Yet, "Sinners in the Hands of an Angry God" is just one of a thousand sermons written and preached by Jonathan Edwards during his pulpit career. Edwards filled most of those sermons with images of joy, love, and God's amazing grace. Edwards also wrote theological essays in an attempt to understand the human religious

2. Calvin, *Institutes*, 3.2.7.

experience. In one such work, "Treatise Concerning Religious Affections," Edwards considers how Christians know the presence of
God in Christ and thus know joy. After distinguishing Christian
joy from the carnal "joys" that debase and corrupt the mind (think
happiness and pleasure), Edwards argues that Christ is the foundation, the content, and the end of our joy. Through the Spirit of God
dwelling in the hearts of the saints, Christians are planted in Christ.
The same Spirit allows Christ's presence to grow in the lives of those
who follow Christ. The Spirit unites the believer with Christ as, day
by day, he or she grows more and more like Christ. Thus, Christians
know joy through their union with Christ himself. Edwards calls
this being a "partaker of God's beauty and Christ's joy."[3]

Joy is fruit of the Spirit. However, joy is not a fruit known
apart from the presence of Christ. When the Spirit dwells in our
hearts we might partake of God's beauty and Christ's joy. In union
with the Father, the Son, and the Holy Spirit, we rejoice *in the Lord*,
always. Yes, to "know" joy is to partake of Christ himself, in mind
and heart, as a miraculous gift.

Receiving a Presence

Christian joy is a *gift* known in Christ's presence. Notice that I did
not say Christians "earn" joy as they "pursue" Christ's presence.
Once learning that joy is known in Christ's presence, all who seek
to know the joy Christ promises are tempted to get to work finding
Christ. Because Christ said he will be with us always, we should
be able to find him if we try hard enough, right? Thus, the endless
quest begins anew.

I once taught a Sunday School class for young adults about
how to keep the Sabbath in the midst of busy lives. Over six weeks
we explored Sabbath not just as a day of rest, but as a lifestyle of
complete dependence upon God. Each week I offered a suggestion
for how participants could practice Sabbath in the week ahead.
These suggestions included things like not spending money for an
entire day, ceasing from worry, noticing where he or she met God

3. Edwards, "Treatise," 158.

each day, and taking time to say "thank you." All wonderful ideas, if I can say so myself. However, after a few weeks, one participant quite rightly protested, saying that while Sabbath was supposed to be about rest, she found herself constantly worrying about whether or not she had done all the things she was supposed to do in order to keep the Sabbath. Her commitment to the wonderful Sabbath practice ideas I suggested actually resulted in the opposite of rest.

We do not need to pursue a God-dependent lifestyle to find the Sabbath. As God's gift to us, the Sabbath is always with us. In a similar way, through our own efforts, we do not know joy. We Christians know joy as a gift. We know joy as we rest in Christ. In the Gospel of John, Jesus himself speaks of this on the night of his betrayal:

> I am the vine and my Father is the vine grower. He removes every branch in me that bears no fruit. Every branch that bears fruit he prunes to make it bear more fruit. You have already been cleansed, by the word that I have spoken to you. *Abide* in me as I abide in you. Just as the branch cannot bear fruit by itself unless it *abides* in the vine, neither can you unless you *abide* in me. I am the vine and you are the branches. Those who *abide* in me and I in them bear much fruit, because apart from me you can do nothing. Whoever does not *abide* in me is thrown away like a branch and withers; such branches are gathered, thrown into the fire, and burned. If you *abide* in me and my words *abide* in you, ask for whatever you wish, and it will be done for you. My Father is glorified by this, that you bear much fruit and become my disciples. As the Father has loved me, so I have loved you; *abide* in my love. If you keep my commandments, you will *abide* in my love just as I have kept my Father's commandments and *abide* in his love. I have said these things to you so that my joy may be in you and that your joy may be complete. (John 15:1–11)

I have quoted this passage in its entirety so that you might notice the operative word—*abide*. Ten times it occurs in this passage. In the midst of his disciples' fear and confusion concerning his departure from them, Jesus does not instruct them to go work hard or get busy with the tasks of ministry. Instead, Jesus tells them to abide in him, just as Jesus himself abides in them.

Abide is not a word that we use all that often anymore. The Greek word *meno* which we translate as "abide" means to rest, to stay, or to set up a tent. For ancient Jews, a primarily nomadic people, to set up a tent meant making a commitment to a single place for an extended period of time. For us today, we might think of abide in terms of when we stop renting a place to live and buy a home. Alternatively, you can think of *abide* as being like coming home at the end of the day, taking off your jacket and kicking off your shoes because you do not plan to go out again that evening. To abide means to stop one's striving and rest. Jesus instructs his disciples to abide in him. So, if we Christians have any hope of faithful discipleship through "bearing fruit," "keeping commandments," and "glorifying God," then we must step back, cease even our busyness for Jesus, and abide in Christ.

The essential gift known by abiding in Christ emerges in the final verse of John 15. Jesus invites the disciples to abide in him, but does so not to make them feel guilty or empower them to work harder. Rather, Jesus shares these things so that "his joy may be in them" and so that "their joy may be complete." Jesus has joy to share and he wants his disciples to know it, to share it, and to have it be complete within them. Jesus wants them to be filled with joy as he is (even on this night of his betrayal!) and to accomplish this he invites them to abide in him. Yes, joy is the gift of Christ himself. It is a free gift. It is not to be earned through work or effort. It is certainly not deserved. It cannot be achieved or even produced. Christ offers his disciples joy as a gift. All that is required is for them to have the faith to stop and rest in him.

Perhaps that is why Alexander Schmemann calls joy "not one of the components of Christianity; it is the *tonality* of Christianity that penetrates everything."[4] Joy is what we know when we realize the truth and the power of God's grace. The Greek word for joy is *chara*, and it is actually derived from the word *charis*, or grace, a gift. Yes, joy is what we discover when we stop trying so hard to

---

4. Schmemann, *Journals*, 137.

find it or create it. Joy is what finds us when we stop taking life so seriously and open ourselves to a little laughter, a little playfulness, and a little lightness of heart.

Ultimately, joy is found not in endless amusement, not in happiness based on pleasant circumstances, but on a cross. Through the cross, God blesses the world by taking upon himself all the busyness, misery, self-indulgence, violence, and quest for control that characterize our lives. In return he gives us the gift of a deep, abiding joy. Through the cross, God blesses the world by destroying our hard-won seriousness and by giving himself to us. We unwrap the gift and find only the crucified and yet risen Christ—joy in our life today and a week from next Tuesday.

Dare we live in such a world, a world in which we find blessing not ultimately in treasured family celebrations, not in second homes at the beach, not in power and being able to overwhelm our enemies, not in amusement we create or leisure we earn, but on a cross? It is a risk to live in such a world. But if we are willing to be surprised by Christ's presence in the ordinary, to receive the amazing gift of grace in a cross and an empty tomb, to join hands with others and celebrate, and to imagine the world as God already sees it, then we might just stumble upon joy in the midst of the ordinary and even the tragic events of our daily life.

Questions for Reflection

1. Are you happy? What kinds of things in your life make you happy?

2. Think about a time when you knew Christ was with you. What was it like? What did you know and experience?

3. Do you prefer to know things with your head and reason or in your heart and emotions?

4. Would you rather give a gift or receive a gift? Why do you think that is the case?

5. When are the times that you most know joy?

2

Christians Have No Joy?

1 Corinthians 13:11–12

"CHRISTIANS HAVE NO JOY." In lectures to students and church members, and in his own writing, Alexander Schmemann claimed that of all the accusations uttered against Christians the most terrible had to be when the nineteenth-century philosopher Friedrich Nietzsche said that Christians have no joy.[1] Today, as tolerance has become the chief virtue in religious and secular dialogue, we might assume the worst accusation against Christians would be that they are judgmental and close-minded. And yet, I think that Schmemann had it right. To say that Christians have no joy is a much more serious charge. Perhaps you are reading this book because you recognize, as I do even in my own life, that this critique contains some truth. There does seem to be a distinct lack of joy in many churches today and in the individual lives of so many Christians. Though we may not be able to articulate exactly what is missing, we believe "there's got to be something more" than what we currently find and know.

In an effort to discover the cause of this malaise we might point to declining and aging church membership or to a culture that no longer even tacitly supports Christian faith and practice. Perhaps the fault lies with worship wars between those who favor traditional worship and those who seek a contemporary expression of faith.

1. Schmemann, *For the Life*, 24.

On the other hand, maybe we should blame shallow preaching that promises that life will be great if you only believe, or that delivers weak proclamations that diminish the gospel's transformative power. Perhaps the cloud of despair comes from lack of programs targeting one generation or multiple generations, or endless denominational arguments over human sexuality and ordination. Wherever you want to point a finger, the result is still the same: without a doubt, the contemporary church lacks the sense of joy.

Yet, as we affirmed in the last chapter, Christ is present in the midst of these trying days. Let us remember that as Christ prepared his disciples for his own death, he promised them the gift of joy. "I will see you again, and your hearts will rejoice, and no one will take your joy from you" (John 16:22). Joy is a gift that cannot be lost or stolen because it is a gift known in Christ's presence. Christ promised not only that he would see us again, but that he would be with us always, even to the end of the age. Thus, the challenge cannot be that Christ is somehow absent from the life of believers. Christ is present just as he promised. And when Christ is present so is the gift of joy.

So the problem for Christians is not how to find Christ or how to create joy. That is not the issue at all. No the problem is one of perception—our inability to perceive and know the joy that is rightfully ours. Christ is here. Joy is present. Yet, our eyes, our minds, and our hearts all miss Christ and the gift of joy he brings. Why might this be the case?

Sin is the simple, and still infinitely complex, answer to any human being's lack of perception. Human beings are sinners. It is our fundamental human condition. Despite redemption in the life, death, and resurrection of Jesus Christ, even Christians struggle with alienation from God. Through both our own efforts and through no fault of our own, we find ourselves distant from God. Instead of perceiving Christ, we see our own self-interest and put our trust in the things of this world. So if we fail to see and notice Christ's presence in our midst, it is because we see through a mirror dimly (1 Cor 13:12).

Yet, in my experience as a pastor, despite our common human sinful condition, most Christians try their best to be good, faithful, and joyful people. We have been deceived into thinking this effort on our part is enough. We keep trying to follow Jesus Christ, even as we fall short. We know that Jesus promised to be with us, and so we do our best to see him. We keep trying to make the Holy Spirit give us the gift of joy. We keep trying to open our eyes, our minds, and our hearts and yet we still cannot seem to perceive Christ's presence or know the gift of joy. We have the best intentions. And by the grace of God, Christ often saves us from even our best intentions.

So, despite our efforts to see clearly, sin appears to cloud our vision. Sin seems to do so in three general ways:

1. We tend to be busy people. Some of our busyness is distraction while much of it entails good and worthwhile things. Yet, even our "busyness for Jesus" can prevent us from noticing Christ's surprising presence.

2. The experience of tragedy threatens to overwhelm us. Suffering and pain, which seem unfair or illogical, lead us to the question, "How can we be joyful when we ourselves and so many others suffer greatly?" Even our heartfelt compassion tends to focus our attention on the hurt rather than on Christ's redeeming presence that is with us always.

3. We often accept without question that we must earn or create all good things. Almost every sphere of our life reinforces the claim that value is defined by achievement. However, to focus on endless earning or creating drastically inhibits our ability to know Christ's transforming presence and receive joy as a gift.

Busyness, the experience of tragedy and suffering, and the rat race to earn and create good things all cloud our vision of Christ. These obstacles prevent us from perceiving Christ's presence with us and thus to knowing the gift of joy that Christ promised. Let us explore each of these areas further.

Busy, Busy, Busy

I once attended a conference in which the keynote speaker asked us to turn over our conference schedule and then write the days of the week across the top of the paper. Under each day, just off the top of our heads, he instructed us to make a list of everything that we did on that day in an average week. Being the diligent and obedient person that I am, I turned my paper over and started writing.

I quickly found that I had some large time blocks for sleep and work. Around these general categories I tried to specify my daily activities, and so I included things like taking the kids to school in the morning, leading Cub Scout dens on Monday night, soccer or baseball practice with the boys on Tuesday and Thursday, Wednesday night dinner and Bible study at church, and mowing the grass on Friday. I added eating breakfast, lunch, and dinner to every day, too, with a bit of a smile.

The speaker then asked us to draw a box around each thing that we considered essential. Things we absolutely had to do. The activities we had no choice but to perform. I drew boxes around sleep, work, prayer, and as much as I hated it, mowing the grass. It just would not do to have a jungle in the backyard.

Next, the speaker asked us to circle the activities that may not be essential to us, but are so important that we did not want to give them up. I circled Cub Scouts, soccer, baseball, taking the kids to school, and so forth. I also found myself circling things like making pancakes or waffles for my family on Saturday morning. Is it essential that I do so? Probably not. And yet, if given a choice between eating out on Saturday morning and cooking at home, I would choose homemade pancakes or waffles every time.

The speaker shared that the exercise was designed to reveal priorities in the midst of busy lives. Yet, when I looked at my paper, I was shocked. Boxes or circles surrounded almost all of my weekly activities.

That exercise illustrates two important aspects of our lives as twenty-first century American followers of Jesus Christ. First, we are busy people and we live in a culture that expects and rewards constant engagement. Very few Christians can be accused of being lazy. Little time for rest appears on the weekly calendar, and if rest does appear we think we must earn it by first completing all our activities and chores. In light of recent economic conditions, those who have managed to hold on to jobs work more days and longer hours. Computers, smartphones, and tablets connect us instantly—not only to information, but also to the demands of work. Planned children's activities have flourished, and my family is not alone in trying to shuttle kids from one commitment to another, every night of the week. When a person is asked a genuine question of concern such as, "How are you?" it is almost a badge of honor to reply with the phrase, "I am busy."

However, examining our daily and weekly activities reveals something even more important about contemporary life. We consider that almost every one of our activities is essential or important. Something that must be done, or is so important that we do not want to give it up, fills most of our days. We choose to invest our time, our financial resources, and our very selves in things that we think matter. If asked to take on additional work or responsibility, or take our child to another educational activity, we will often just add the additional load without giving up anything else. And why would we? We perceive everything we do as being essential or important. However, soon we find that there are not enough hours in the day for all the worthwhile things that seek our attention. There is hardly any blank space on the calendar. Yet, as our busyness grows more impressive so does our stress, frustration, and discontent. We might not always name it as such, but I think we would best call this experience "despair."

All this and we have not even talked about busyness with our faith and the church. We think we must be doing everything right when we are busy for Jesus! We read our Bibles every day and we come to church for worship each Sunday (or we have an excellent excuse why we missed). We volunteer with the soup kitchen and help teach Sunday School. We will be there to decorate for Vacation Bible School and help wash dishes in the kitchen on Wednesday nights. We will go on the Mission Trip with the youth and we give our money (often quite generously). We do so much ministry and mission wonderfully right, and we participate in these essential practices to nourish our faith. However, our spirits grow heavy and we fall exhausted.

For even our "busyness for Jesus" can sinfully cloud our vision. As we rush from one activity to another, we often fail to perceive

Christ's presence with us and the gift of joy Christ brings. In the midst of our busyness, is it possible to be surprised by joy and to glimpse Christ even in the ordinary?

So Many People Suffer

My aunt and uncle own a lake cottage in upstate New York. For years the entire Rich family would attempt to converge on the cottage each summer for a week in August. Living in North Carolina, it was often the only time of year I was able to see my grandparents, my aunts and uncles, and my cousins.

As we all grew busier it became harder and harder for everyone to make it to the lake. However, in the summer of 2002 somehow the entire family was there. My grandfather's health was beginning to wane, but his mind was as sharp as ever. I remember clearly one particular afternoon, sitting on the deck with my grandfather, whom we called Poppy, and several of my cousins and their spouses. Poppy asked us what we thought was the most significant event that had happened in our lifetime. When we moved out of the personal experiences of marriage and childbirth, the event we all returned to was the September 11th attack on the World Trade Center and the Pentagon a year before. As young adults in our late 20s or early 30s, we could all clearly recall where we were when we first heard the news.

I was driving in my car, passing through downtown Monroe, North Carolina, where Sarah and I lived, on my way to the church I served in Pageland, South Carolina. Listening to National Public Radio, I heard a report that a small private plane had crashed into one of the Twin Towers in New York City. Moments later, the report changed—the plane had been a commercial jet. I called Sarah, who was pregnant with our first child, on my cell phone—the first cell phone I had ever owned. Then the report came of the other plane hitting the other tower. More reports: a plane had plunged into the Pentagon and another fell into a Pennsylvania field.

I reached the church. Once inside, I watched news coverage on a television, by myself, in the church fellowship hall. I planned a prayer service with the neighboring Methodist pastor. That night we gathered in our sanctuary to pray and to talk about what kinds of supplies we could gather for the victims. We also shared information about an upcoming blood drive—that was before we knew there would be so little need for donated blood. As Sarah and I lay in bed that night we held each other tight and wondered about the kind of world into which we were bringing a child.

That afternoon, almost a year later, Poppy reminded us that each generation can point to a particular day or event as their significant common experience—a day that changed their world. For one generation it might be Neil Armstrong's first step on the moon, for another it might be the assassination of President John F. Kennedy. For another generation it might be the attack on Pearl Harbor that led the United States into World War II. For still another generation it might have been the 1929 stock market collapse and the beginning of the Great Depression. I am confident that the generations following us will each know the common experience of a day that changes their world.

For my cousins and me, we lost a bit of our collective innocence on September 11, 2001. Tragedy had hit close to home that day. Today's twenty-four-hour news channels and Internet make it hard for us to bury our heads in the sand. Even the statistics on tragedy and suffering can easily overwhelm us. Millions of children in the United States live in poverty; more than 20,000 children around the world die of preventable diseases every day; more than a billion people live in the world on less than one dollar a day. If we stop for a moment and consider all the tragedy in the world, and the number of people who suffer, despair quickly threatens our personal sense of well-being. We must ask: How can there be joy in a world when so many people suffer?

While the worldwide scope of tragedy and suffering can be overwhelming, it is my experience that the majority of those people who seek pastoral counsel do so because they experience the sort of suffering that is much closer to home. The questions asked are far more personal. How can I know joy when I suffer? How can I know joy when I watch those I love suffer? For all it takes is one suspicious text on your boyfriend's phone. One bag of marijuana found hidden beneath your child's mattress. One friend laid off from work. One argument at church that ends in tears. One late night call that sends you to the emergency room. One person in your family diagnosed with cancer. One night wide awake in bed because the one you love will never lay her head on the other pillow again. All it takes is one.

Whether it is thousands, millions, billions, or just one event, tragedy threatens to overwhelm us. With our eyes open to those in such need, tears naturally cloud our vision. How can Christ be present in the midst of such pain? How can we know the gift of joy when so many suffer? How may we experience the joy of resurrection in our own lives today?

Hi Ho, Hi Ho, It's Off to Work We Go

"What kind of work do you do?" Where I live that is the question you ask when you meet someone new. This question is quickly followed by, "Where do you go to church?" and "Tell me who your mother was." In a small Southern town we assume that everyone goes to church (even though we recognize many do not). We also know that you can tell a lot about a person if you know their family (i.e., not who their mother *is*, but who she *was*). Yet, even in the South we begin getting to know someone by asking about their job.

However, awkwardness fills the room if the individual replies, "I'm laid off" or "I'm looking." If the individual has left the workforce to focus on being a parent, the person will often fill the awkward silence by sharing what he or she used to do.

Such is the way that we allow paid work to define our identity. In the face of difficult times when so many people have lost jobs, we tend to celebrate opportunities to work and individuals who have a willingness to work hard. In my pastoral ministry, I meet men and women in their late fifties who have lost jobs due to downsizing. Many possess adequate resources to retire, but do not feel as if they have earned the ability to do so, or that they have achieved enough to provide for a comfortable future. They believe they need to work.

On the other end of the spectrum, a recent study indicated that more than 50 percent of college graduates under the age of twenty-five are currently unemployed or underemployed.[2] Student loans and credit card debt threaten these young graduates and their financial futures. They want to work and feel lost without a job.

A theological problem emerges as work begins to define human identity and worth. When we believe our value as a person depends upon our ability to achieve at work, succeed at school, or excel on the sports field, it is easy to believe that in every sphere of our life we must create or earn all good things. Despite the gospel message of grace, the church so often operates in exactly the same way. Think for a minute about the members of your church that you most admire? Who are the men and women who would you nominate for a leadership position? Did you think first of the person who only comes to worship once a month, sits on the back row, and never says anything to anyone? Or did your mind come to rest on an individual who is very involved with worship, Sunday School, Bible Study, and serving on a committee or two or three? At least in the churches I know, if God is calling you to be a leader, you better have earned that position through hard work. It is no wonder that so many are overwhelmed by being "busy for Jesus."

At our jobs, at home, at school, in athletics, and even in the church we hear and experience the fact that if we want the good life, if we want to be happy, then we have to work hard. You, as an individual, cannot depend upon anyone else to provide for your needs, so the burdens of the world fall squarely on your shoulders. There is little time for jokes, laughter, and joy because there is too much work to be done.

In joining this "rat race" we buy into the assumption that we must earn or create all good things. Yet this way of life clouds our vision of joy. If everything depends upon us, then we will fail to see Christ present in our brothers and sisters in faith and the celebrations we might share with them. If we must earn or create all good things through our own hard work, we will not see that joy is a gift, and that a future of security might be received but will never be achieved. Is it possible to see clearly, to join hands, and together expect the fulfillment of Christ's promise?

2. Yen, "1 in 2 new graduates," para. 2.

The Gift of Christ's Presence

While Nietzsche's claim that Christians have no joy contains some truth, it does not describe the whole story. Busyness, tragedy and suffering, and the quest to earn or create all good things can all cloud our vision. However, even these obstacles cannot ultimately obscure Christ's presence with us and the gift of joy that Christ brings. Christ's promise is true.

So how do we find the joy we seek to see and know? Unfortunately, because joy is a gift it cannot be forced. Instead of a three-step plan or a series of commitments that guarantee you more joy, I can only point you to places where you might perceive joy because Christ is present there. In fact, I want to suggest to you that Christ's own life is a window through which you might begin to see Christ's presence and thus know joy in your life today and even a week from next Tuesday.

Just as Christ's birth takes place in the most unusual of places for a king, joy often surprises us in the most unusual and sometimes inopportune moments in our lives.

Just as Christ calls his first disciples while they are at work, takes them to their hometowns, and teaches them with parables and examples from daily life, so too can we experience joy in the ordinary events of work, family, community, and church.

For the sake of the joy that was set before him, Christ endured the cross and declared that a thief would be with him in paradise. So too in the midst of tragedy and suffering we might know the gift of joy and Christ's presence with us.

On the third day, Christ was raised from the tomb and made a mockery of death. Likewise, joy releases us from the bonds of sin and death as we experience the comedy of resurrection.

After his resurrection, Christ gathered with discouraged disciples in Emmaus and on the shore of the Sea of Galilee to share a joyful feast with them. As we gather around the table with brothers and sisters in Christ, we too might know the joy and gift of Christ in community.

Christ has promised to come again to create all things new, and in that day God's home will be with mortals. Even as all the temporal pleasures and happiness we earn and create fade away, Christ's gift of joy will remain as we long for that day.

Glimpses of Joy

In the six chapters that follow in this book, we will explore Christ's birth, life and ministry, death, resurrection, appearances, and promised return as an opportunity to discover the gift of joy in the midst of the surprising, ordinary, and tragic moments in our own lives. I love to tell stories, so you will learn more about times in which I have known joy. But as I conclude this chapter, I want to share with you some glimpses of the places where I have noticed Christ's gift of joy even in the midst of the busyness, tragedy, and culture of achievement that mark my own life. I pray that these glimpses of joy might help you begin to notice this great gift in your own life, too.

I visited with a young mother in the hospital who gave birth to her second child, a daughter. Her husband would not return from military service in Kuwait until the next month.

In my home, there is a five-year-old little girl who stands on her bed, music blaring from her Princess CD player, as she rocks out at the top of her lungs with her microphone.

One of her big brothers loves to watch every sport on television, and every five minutes calls out, "Daddy, Daddy, did you know . . ."

There is her other big brother who plays the piano and the trumpet and fills our house with beautiful music.

There is my wife Sarah, who throughout fifteen years of marriage has always known exactly the moments when I need a word of reassurance and the moments when I need a word of challenge, and she's not afraid to tell me both because she loves me that much.

There is the church member who faced a life-threatening illness and remarked, "I'm grateful for the aches and pains because I almost didn't get to feel anything anymore."

There is a 104-year-old member of our congregation who cannot hear or see, but still rides the church bus to worship every time she remembers it is Sunday.

There is the chance I had, surrounded by family and their friends, to speak words of hope and joy at a service of witness to the resurrection for my grandfather, Poppy, and my grandmother, Gram.

There is a group of preschoolers and me during the Time with Children spinning around the chancel every time we sing the word, "rejoice." The song ends, the children lie down on the floor dizzy and my head is so swimming that I almost miss my little stool.

That same Sunday, there is a group of deacons in the narthex as the congregation sings to conclude the service. Every time they sing the word, "rejoice," the deacons dance in a circle, hands in the air, huge smiles upon their faces.

Yes, joy—the real presence of Christ known in the midst of both laughter and tears. Can you see it? It is Christ's gift to you today and even a week from next Tuesday.

Questions for Reflection

1. If you feel like there's got to be something more at your church, what reasons would you give for what's missing? Have you ever thought that the missing ingredient might be joy?

2. In your own life, how do you find your vision clouded by busyness, tragedy and suffering, or feeling like you must earn or create all good things?

3. Use the chart in the Appendix of this book to make a list of everything you do during an average week. Have you ever thought that you are "too busy for Jesus"? How might you create space in your life in the midst of so many essential and important commitments?

4. Do you tend to ignore or become overwhelmed by tragedy and suffering?

5. How caught up are you in the "rat race" to earn and create good things for you and your family?

3

Stumbling Upon Joy

Luke 2:8–39

TINA FEY IS BUSY. This actress and comedienne first achieved celebrity status as the head writer and host of the news segment on *Saturday Night Live*. Then she started writing and acting in movies. Next, she wrote, starred in, and produced a television show called *30 Rock* about a sketch comedy show much like *Saturday Night Live*. She got married. She became a mom. She wrote a book. Everyone knew Tina Fey. Tina was busy.

About this time, Tina starred in a television commercial for the credit card company American Express.[1] In the one-minute ad, Tina steps off an elevator, apparently at work, and people immediately start asking her to make decisions. Reviewing scripts as she walks down the hall, she says they need some German Shepherds for one sketch. A woman calls her name saying that she needs Tina over here. From the other direction a man holding two flutes approaches her. Tina plays one and chooses the other. She walks down a hall when someone shouts that her daughter said it was octopus time.

We see Tina running to catch a cab. Next is a quick shot of Tina sitting in a tiny chair across from a two-year-old at a day care. Tina is waving a blue plush octopus and making a funny noise. She jumps back into the cab again. She arrives at the office to find a group of men with funny hats and shepherd's crooks. She shakes

1. *Tina Fey American Express*, no page.

her head and says she meant the other kind of German Shepherds. Her phone rings as she runs into her office. Answering on speakerphone, she hears a pleasant voice from American Express asking if she purchased 14,000 racquetballs. Visibly annoyed, Tina says that she did not purchase 14,000 racquetballs. The voice replies, "No problem, we'll take it off your account right away."

Tina starts to sit back in her chair and asks, "You mean I don't have to do anything?" The voice replies, "Nope." As Tina leans back, a smile creeps across her face and she takes a drink of coffee. Her assistant runs in declaring that the writers' room is on fire, and Tina sprints out after her with the fire extinguisher . . .

For one brief moment in an incredibly busy day, a day in which everything seemed to depend on her, Tina Fey received a gift. This lone gift produced her only smile. Something like joy surprised this busy woman who was trying to do it all herself.

My good friend Tom Currie, an experienced pastor and dean of Union Presbyterian Seminary at Charlotte, says this about joy: "Such a gift, far from being a positive attitude or constantly upbeat mood, is best described as a deep confidence, even a kind of astonished laughter because of the discovery that there is One at work in our world more central to our stories than we are to ourselves. Such joy is always a surprise."[2]

The Surprising Nature of Christian Joy

Such joy is always a surprise, especially in the midst of our busy lives. Consider the time when an angel of the Lord appeared to shepherds living in the fields, keeping watch over their flocks by night: "Do not be afraid; for see—I am bringing you good news of great joy for all the people: to you is born this day in the city of David a Savior, who is the Messiah, the Lord. This will be a sign for you: you will find a child wrapped in bands of cloth and lying in a manger" (Luke 2:10–12).

Wow! This is certainly not news these shepherds expected to learn as they gathered their sheep, started a fire, cooked their

2. Currie, *Joy of Ministry*, 3–4.

dinner, and readied themselves for a night under the stars. Their greatest hope for the night was probably not to lose any sheep. Not losing sheep demanded their persistence and diligence. Shepherds are kept pretty busy because sheep like to wander off and predators are always on the lookout for easy prey. Were these shepherds anticipating angels and announcements about the birth of the Messiah? Not likely.

So, to say the least, this good news surprises these shepherds. In this angelic announcement of Christ's birth, you and I today can find at least two surprises connected with the "great joy." We should expect that the Messiah's birth should be good news of great joy to these shepherds. This is no surprise to us. We know that generations and generations of people had been eagerly expecting the arrival of a Messiah. Again, no surprise for us here. But what surprises us in this announcement is both the recipients of this good news and the sign of its veracity.

We would expect that good news of the Messiah's birth would be announced to those of power and importance. Kings, rulers, priests, and leaders of the synagogue seem likely choices. And yet, the angel appears to shepherds keeping watch over their flocks by night. These were not the wealthy or the powerful or the important. Shepherds were hired hands, common people who slept beneath the stars. They worked with their hands. They were the salt of the earth—normal everyday folks. It is surprising that *to them* this good news of great joy comes.

Then the sign that the shepherds receive should also surprise us, as it did them. Recall that the shepherds are told that they will find "a child wrapped in bands of cloth and lying in a manger." The news astonished these shepherds. The Messiah who has come to save God's people is born in a manger? Surely not in such a common and lowly place! But why should this news also surprise us? Let me start by saying that our celebrations of Jesus' birth at Christmas are often glamorous and slick productions. Conversely, kids in bathrobes make us smile as they act out the scenes in the Christmas play. But have you ever taken a step back to really think about what the birth of Jesus was like?

My wife Sarah collects nativity scenes. Each year on the Friday after Thanksgiving I go up to the attic, pull down the plastic crates of Christmas decorations, and begin unwrapping and placing various crèches around the house. We have some simple ones with just Mary, Joseph, and baby Jesus. Others include cute cotton ball sheep and handcrafted donkeys. However, my favorite nativity scene takes a little longer to unwrap and place because it includes Mary, Joseph, Jesus, an angel, the innkeeper, a stable, three wise men, two shepherds, multiple sheep, cows, a donkey, and even a camel.

Each year as I unwrap that elaborate nativity scene I am struck by how busy and noisy and smelly Jesus' birth must have been. No sterile birthing room, complete with whirlpool spa for Mary. Jesus, the Son of God, the long awaited Messiah, was born in the midst of a busy, noisy, smelly stable. He was then wrapped in swaddling clothes, which is little more than a piece of cloth, and was then laid in a manger, that is, a food trough for livestock. All this does not immediately call to mind the majestic chorus of "Joy to the World" and certainly raises questions about the claim, "no crying he makes." The Messiah is born in a stable and laid in a manger. He was delivered to the care and witness of common folk. Most unexpected. But such is the surprising nature of the incarnation of God with us.

A Papier-Mâché Flamingo

Yes, Christ tends to appear in the most unexpected moments, and we often find joy in the most surprising places. Not long ago I attended a workshop where I had a chance to meet a pastor named Craig Goodwin. Craig lives in Spokane, Washington, with his wife, Nancy, and their two children; both girls are slightly older than my own kids. Two days after Christmas in 2007, Craig and Nancy were fed up with the whole holiday experience of spending lots of money for so little happiness and joy. So, over a bowl of soup in a Thai restaurant, on the back of a comment card, they made a pledge that in 2008 they would live much more intentionally. As a concrete expression of this pledge, they committed to limiting their purchases and consumption to things that were local, used, home-grown, and homemade. This was a big step for the Goodwins. They are a regular, suburban middle-class family. They live in a midsize city, in a housing development where the residents care about their neighborhood. They are a lot like my family, and maybe a lot like yours, too.

Craig tells the story of that year in his family's life in a book called *Year of Plenty*. It is a fascinating tale, and Craig tells it with great honesty. Suffice it to say that he and his family found it hard to drastically change their purchasing habits with little to no prepara-tion. For example, is the toilet paper that you use in your house locally made, or if not local then handmade, homegrown, or used? I certainly hope it is not used.

If my own family were to try to live more simply in this way, one of the greatest challenges would be birthday parties. With three children, it seems that we go to a birthday party every weekend of the year. Our busy schedule usually means a quick trip to Walmart to buy a $15 plastic toy or a gift card. However, both of those gifts were off limits for Craig and Nancy when their girls received a birth-day party invitation. And when the first of their own girls' birthdays arrived less than a month into their experiment, everything for the party had to be homemade, including a flamingo piñata.

The Internet provides plentiful information for such an en-deavor, so the day before the party Craig and the girls set out to cre-ate their flamingo with two spheres, a larger one for the body and another smaller one for the head. The spheres were formed using balloons. A cardboard tube neck connected the spheres. Additional tube legs extended from the bottom sphere. Layer upon layer of newspaper and magazine strips coated in homemade plaster, which was made from flour and water, covered the balloons for the body and head. After two hours of work and multiple fine tunings to en-sure it stood on its own two feet, Craig and the girls cleaned up their mess and went off to bed.

The morning of the birthday party arrived and, by the grace of God, the flamingo still stood. Yet, in their efforts to ensure the body would hold its shape, they had added too many layers of papier-mâché. It was not dry. A hair dryer did little to speed up the process, so with the hour of the party rapidly approaching, they got out a needle to pop the balloons.

The balloon in the body slowly deflated and the wet newspaper collapsed with it. Tears and running out of the room quickly followed. Craig writes: "Our five hours of work and preparation were literally collapsing before our eyes. It was a catastrophe. A daughter's simple wishes for a good birthday crushed, a father stuck in the worst kind of night-before-Christmas-toy-assembly nightmare, and a mother too stressed out about her made-from-scratch birthday cake decorated with leftover Halloween candy to pay attention."[3]

The experiment in simple living almost came to a halt. And yet, in this moment, which would become a routine part of their year, they were surprised by joy. With no other option, Craig popped the balloon in the flamingo's head and incredibly, it maintained its shape. Hearing this news, his daughter slowly came back into the room. They decided to fill the head with candy and the body with newspaper. Who would know that they hadn't planned it exactly this way?

When the guests arrived, the intact flamingo stood, unpainted and undecorated. Later hung from the banister, no one noticed its unsightly appearance as the blindfolded kids all took turns whacking the bird. When the head finally flew off after a vigorous hit and candy scattered everywhere, the kids cheered and descended to claim their prizes.

It was not a simple day by any means. Craig calls it stressful, complex, exhausting, and inefficient. And yet, when he asked his daughter how she liked her party, without any prompting, she said that her favorite part was the piñata. Not just the chaos of gathering candy but the time of preparing and overcoming adversity together. Behold the surprising gift of joy.

---

3. Goodwin, *Year of Plenty*, 43.

Dancing in the Temple

Birthday parties are a way of marking the passage of time. In the midst of our busy lives, we try to stop and celebrate even though throwing a party often adds more stress to our lives.

We celebrate another birthday of sorts when we mark the end of one year and the beginning of the next. Instead of wrapped presents, and the occasional homemade flamingo piñata, at a New Year's celebration we often find an image of a long-bearded old man who is holding a baby. Each one wears a sash: the old man's sash is embroidered with the year that has just ended and the baby's with the year just begun. Often slumped and resting on a cane, the old man carries all the burdens and sorrows of the year past. Bright eyed and eager, the child holds all the hopes and dreams of a year to come. An old man and a baby—expected symbols of the progression of time that we mark with the turn of a calendar page.

Let us return to the surprising story of shepherds and angels that surround Jesus' birth. The second chapter of the Gospel of Luke next shares with us a family trip to the temple (Luke 2:22–39). There is a lot to say about the various Jewish laws and ritual observances that Luke shares with us. Certainly, we could discuss the piety of Mary and Joseph as they raised the Son of God. The example they set is laudable and is an appropriate model for those of us raising children today. However, ultimately, this passage in Luke, a story about a trip to the temple, is a story about an old man and an old woman, Simeon and Anna, who prepared themselves to see the Messiah and know joy, and yet experienced surprise as they gazed into the eyes of an eight-day-old child.

Have you ever held such a young life in your arms? It is a powerful moment, to be sure. Once you pass through the fear and anxiety about dropping the child and make sure you properly support the head, you begin the innate rocking motions of back and forth, back and forth. Within that rocking rhythm is an opportunity to gaze and wonder. What will a week from next Tuesday hold for the little life now wrapped securely in a blanket? What will she become when she grows up? How tall will he be? Will her eyes stay blue? Will he smile and laugh in a life of levity? Will she weep and rage in a life of sorrow? What will a week from next Tuesday hold for this little life now resting in your arms?

It does not matter if it is your child, or your grandchild, or a child of the church, or the child of a stranger noticed just in passing, the questions are still the same. Those who God blesses with the chance to watch children grow know that one day all those questions will be answered. One day this child in your arms will be an adult and the future will be the present. Their height and eye color will be fixed, their smiles and laughter, their tears and rage will all be known. Perhaps they too will hold a child in their arms. But all of that is to come, for in the moment, rocking back and forth, we only gaze with wonder, hope, and dreams.

Thus, it was for Simeon and Anna. I wish we had a picture of this scene as Simeon took the child Jesus in his arms and praised God. All we have is his words, but my hunch is that the scene would not resemble the image of the old man and the baby we see at the end of a calendar year. Instead of an old man slumped by burdens and sorrows, we would see a man whose youthful vigor has returned. For Simeon had spent his life preparing and expecting and "looking forward to the consolation of Israel." He was always gazing into the future, always with expectant hope for the one who was promised, for the one who was coming, for the one who would be the "salvation which God had prepared in the presence of all peoples." A life spent looking forward while living in hope was now complete. The fulfillment of Simeon's great longing to be in the presence of Christ was not a moment of weariness and resignation, but of joy and song and praise.

In the same way, the prophetess Anna, eighty-four years young, joined him in his song. For in that moment, she too came to see the child Jesus and began to praise God and to speak about him "to all who were looking for the redemption of Israel." Mother and father stand by amazed, and no wonder. Think of the looks and the whispers throughout the temple—an old man and an old woman singing and praising and maybe even dancing with a child in their arms.

But what will become of this child? Instead of being bright eyed and eager, full of unlimited possibility and dreams, this child carries the burden of generations. He is the one who will save Israel. But salvation and consolation do not come without great cost. Yes, this child is "a light for revelation to the Gentiles and for glory to the people Israel;" but "He is also destined for the falling and rising of many in Israel and to be a sign that will be opposed so that the inner thoughts of many will be revealed" (Luke 2:32–34). Because of him, a sword will pierce the soul of his mother.

Simeon and Anna had prepared themselves well. While we cannot create or produce the moment in which we will experience the physical presence of Christ, just like Simeon and Anna did, we can prepare ourselves to perceive God at work. And yet, even as we prepare, joy still surprises us. Simeon and Anna saw all that was to come for this child. It was a vision of salvation that was neither a utopian fantasy nor a fairy tale. Everyone would not live happily ever after. But they sang and danced. For one day the child would be an adult and the future would be the present. His height and eye color fixed; his smiles and laughter, his tears and rage would be known. He too would hold a child in his arms and say that anyone who wanted to enter the kingdom of God must become like this. A supper, an arrest, a trial, a cross, an empty tomb. All of that was to come. But gazing in the child's eyes, Simeon and Anna saw that it was already there. Joy, the unexpected gift of Christ himself, rested in their arms, and an old man and an old woman sang and danced.

What Happens in Mexico . . .

Singing and dancing did not cross my mind as I arrived at the airport on the Monday after Easter. No, I was in a bad mood. The week between Palm Sunday and Easter Sunday had been especially busy that year. I prepared for and led seven worship services, preached six sermons, and taught five Bible studies that week. My son Sam had surgery to remove his tonsils a week before, and then woke up in the middle of the night with bleeding in his throat that required a trip back to the hospital. I worried that he was not yet well. I had received comments back from my doctor of ministry thesis advisors but did not have time to make the revisions they requested or set up the day and time for my final evaluation. I was exhausted. Yet being tired after Holy Week was typical for a busy pastor in a growing and busy church.

In response to the exhaustion of Holy Week, I usually take a week off. This little vacation gives me space to step back from my professional duties and spend more time with my family. However, that year, instead of relaxing on the beach somewhere, I was getting on a plane to Mexico. For twelve years in a row, members of our church had traveled to Reynosa, Mexico, in partnership with Faith Ministry to build houses and work with residents in the poorest sections of the city. Many of our members had known transformational experiences on this trip. I felt that, as the pastor of First Presbyterian Church, I needed to personally support this important mission of our church.

I was still in a bad mood when my flight arrived at the airport in McAllen, Texas. This bad mood darkened as I waited to be picked up by our group. An hour passed. They had been delayed at the border. They arrived. But my foul mood did not abate. I was exhausted, unhappy, and inconvenienced. I felt like I was there because I had to be there. And away we went, bound for Reynosa.

But somewhere along the way, Christ surprised me.

Joy kept showing up because Jesus kept showing up in Mexico. He was definitely not there in the rooster that crowed to wake us up at 4:00 a.m. But he showed up Tuesday morning in one of the youth's, Anderson, smiley faces in the cement we mixed; he showed up in the one row of cement block that Robert and I struggled for hours to lay and keep level; and he definitely showed up in David's relief when he finally found the lost keys to the van. He was there when Linda and Katherine made bracelets while surrounded by Mexican children. Christ was there.

Jesus showed up on Tuesday night as Kathy and Doug invited each member of our team to share how another member had made a difference that day. He appeared in Jim and Don's safe and careful driving through sometimes crowded, often bumpy, bumpy, streets in Reynosa. He definitely was present when Charlotte, Kelly, Morgan, Katherine, Linda, and Linda painted little girls' fingernails on Wednesday afternoon in Naranjito. Yes, Christ was there.

He was in Renie's deep love for the Mexican people, in her translation of the foreman's instructions from Spanish into English, and in her careful planning and leadership of our trip. No doubt about it, Christ showed up when Don, with his vast experience in engineering and construction, told David and me that our job of tying rebar together was important, but not "structurally essential." On the day we poured a roof, when Linda handed me empty buckets as I knelt under the scaffolding, waiting to set them out to be filled again, he was there. In my aching back, shoulders, and knees at the end of each day, Christ was there.

In Kelly's shoveling, Charlotte's mixing, Doug's wheelbarrows full of sand and gravel, Robert's buckets of water, and Morgan's placing the buckets so they could be filled and I could lift them on the day we poured the floor, Christ was there.

I am not exactly sure when he showed up, but Christ was definitely there when we made lunch each day for our Mexican *amigos*. He was there on Thursday morning when we all carved our names in a cement plaque on the wall of Juanita's new addition. He surprised me on Friday afternoon when Pastor Alfredo asked me to come forward and pray a Prayer of Dedication for the new homes built that week, tears in the eyes of the new homeowners and in my own as well. Christ was definitely there when final good-byes were shared with Mexican friends, old and new, and promises were made to see one another again. Yes, Christ showed up and I knew joy.

This joy was not simple levity, amusement, or happiness. It did not consist of just an uplift of my spirit or a moment of peace in great busyness, for the pain and poverty of that community did not permit such emotions. Still, I saw Christ in the people, in the place, and in even myself as my bad mood turned to gratitude. I knew the power of resurrection and new life. As our hosts sang songs at evening chapel, my heart heard and knew Christ's background music—joy.

There is a saying that "What happens in Mexico, stays in Mexico." But what happened in Mexico that week did not stay in Mexico. Christ showed up and surprised us with joy, every day. And today I am filled with great joy because I am able to share that story with you.

A busy comedienne is surprised by grace. In much the same way, Christ keeps surprising us in a Messiah's birth in a stable announced to shepherds watching their flock by night, in a homemade flamingo piñata, in an old man and an old woman's dance and song, and in an exhausted pastor working in Mexico the week after Easter. Today, tomorrow, and a future joy keeps showing up because Christ keeps showing up.

Questions for Reflection

1. Do you tend to try to do everything yourself? Share a time when you received an unexpected gift. How did you respond?

2. As you imagine being there with the shepherds watching their flocks by night, what surprises you most about the story of Jesus' birth?

3. Simeon and Anna spent years waiting, watching, and preparing to see the Messiah. How might you prepare yourself to see Jesus in the midst of your busy life today?

4. Share a time in which you were surprised by noticing Christ's presence with you. How did it change things for you?

5. Why do you think that joy so often surprises us?

4

Joy in Seconds

Mark 1:14–21

"HELLO. MAY I SPEAK with Bobby?" I asked one Tuesday evening in March.

"You got him, but everyone calls me Possum," replied the voice on the other end of the phone.

"Okay, ah . . . Possum . . . my name is Matt Rich and I'm going to be your son Zachary's baseball coach this spring. We are the Rangers."

"Have you ever coached before?" Possum asked.

"Well, I've not coached coach-pitch baseball before. I did watch my older son play two seasons and my younger son Sam play in the fall. I've also coached soccer for the last six years and T-ball for the last four years."

"So I guess it was time for you to move up."

"I guess so," I replied. "Our first practice is going to be on Friday night at 6 p.m. Zachary will need a glove. Most of the kids will wear cleats and get their own bat, but those are not required. If you have any questions, please give me a call."

"Okay, we'll see you Friday," Possum said. "By the way, Zachary goes by Gus."

I must say that at first I was not sure I wanted to coach baseball for seven- and eight-year-olds. The kids were not the cause of my concern. In fact, I enjoy coaching youth soccer. My fellow soccer coaches and I often comment that it is easy to coach soccer in Robeson County, North Carolina, because none of the parents believe their son is going to be the next Landon Donovan or Wayne Rooney. But baseball—baseball—is another matter. Everyone *knows* that his or her son is the next Derek Jeter or Albert Pujols (if he's not there already)! Coaching youth baseball can be as much about controlling overzealous parents' expectations about playing time and winning as it is about keeping the players focused on the game and not hitting each other with bats in the dugout!

It's also a significant time commitment to coach baseball. First Presbyterian Church, Lumberton, is a growing, busy, and often demanding—in a very good way—congregation. So to commit at least two nights a week and most Saturdays for four months to coaching baseball was a serious matter for me. In any event, it required me to dedicate a lot of time to something other than my family and the church.

But my son Sam really wanted me to coach. So I, as they say in Scripture, "girded up my loins" and kept making phone calls.

A Visitor on the Job

If you have already used the form in this book's Appendix to list the various activities that occupy your time during a normal week, I want you to take another look at it. Look over the days of that week, and then make a guess about how much time each week you spend inside your church. Recent studies have shown that even the most faithful and dedicated Christians spend approximately 5 percent of their week inside the walls of their church.[1] That means on average, you spend 95 percent of your life not at church. Christians are busy for Jesus at church, but the vast majority of their time is spent in the world.

I call this 95 percent of our lives, "a week from next Tuesday." This is just normal, regular, ordinary life. The day to day events of living that occupy the majority of our time. A week from next Tuesday we will be at home, at the grocery store, at restaurants, at the park, in the car, at the baseball field, at work. This is where we spend

1. "What is My 95?," para. 2.

our time. Jesus spent his time there, too. And wherever Jesus shows up, and we notice, there is joy.

Jesus himself grew up in a small town; he worked with his hands as a tradesman and carpenter. Jesus understood the truth and necessity and value of everyday work. Although he grew up in a faithful family, he spent much of his early days of public ministry where we, too, spend our time. He went out in the world to meet people, embrace his calling, and then gather his first disciples. And where did all of his occur? According to Mark, not at church.

In Mark, we quickly learn about John the Baptizer who prepared the way for the Messiah. We read about Jesus' baptism by John, and the voice from heaven declaring to Jesus, "You are my son, the Beloved; with you I am well pleased." Just two quick verses describe Jesus in the wilderness where he was tempted. Then suddenly we learn that after John has been arrested, Jesus returns to Galilee proclaiming good news and announcing that the kingdom of God has drawn near. As soon as Jesus starts telling people about the kingdom of God he begins inviting individuals to be a part of it.

And where do you think he starts looking for people to join him? Does he go to the synagogue? I understand there was a very nice synagogue in Capernaum at this time. But no. Does he consult with the rabbis so he might find the best students? Nope. How about the other religious leaders, scribes, or Pharisees? No again. Jesus doesn't look in any of the "churchy" or religious places at all. Instead, he goes to visit some men at work.

If you have heard the story of Jesus calling his first disciples, you will never forget it. If you have never read this story, you need to put down this book, go find a Bible, and read Mark 1:14–20 right now.

Imagine Jesus walking by the Sea of Galilee. Try to picture this scene in your mind. For most of my life I always saw this event bathed in sunshine. There was Jesus walking beside the Sea of Galilee, smiling with a bird sitting on his shoulder singing "zip-a-dee-doo-dah." It is always sunny when Jesus is around, right?

If that is your mental image of this scene too, put it aside for a moment and try to picture it a little differently. Imagine that the clouds have rolled down off the hills and a light mist fills the air.

Jesus walks down the shore and comes across Simon and Andrew who are casting a net into the sea. They are professional, although small-time, fishermen who have been hardened and tanned by their work outdoors every day. Suppose it is a bad day for these fishermen. They haven't caught enough fish to cover their expenses. They were expected at home an hour ago because someone had brought word that Simon's mother-in-law suffered from a fever. Their net catches on a log and rips. Curses on their breath, they wade out to free the net, and then haul it back in. This is not one of those days when the nets are bursting. It's the sort of work day that amounts to a lot of labor and no pay. This is a week from next Tuesday sort of day. It's one of those days the fishermen work because they *have* to work.

On a day like that, while they are hard at work, Jesus shows up. He calls them and immediately they drop everything and follow him.

A little farther down the shore, Jesus comes across a slightly larger operation, a family business we might say. Try to imagine this scene on the same day—the same clouds, the same mist. James and John, the sons of Zebedee, are in a boat mending the nets. They must have been doing pretty well to have boats for fishing. Maybe there had been a good-sized catch recently that tattered their nets. Yes, a pretty good-sized catch—that was great. Yet, they also had all the pretty good-sized headaches that come with running a family business. They had inventory to complete, profits to distribute, more work to do than time in which to do it, and don't get them started on what it was like to work for Dad.

On a day like that, while they are at work, Jesus shows up. He calls them and immediately they too drop everything and follow him.

Is this a story with which you can identify? Do you expect that Jesus is going to show up where you work on Monday morning? What might happen if you did start expecting Jesus to be present at work? For just as the angels greeted shepherds watching their flocks by night with news of great joy at Jesus' birth, Jesus himself appears in the middle of a workday for these fishermen by the Sea of Galilee and offers them the gift of joy if only they will follow him.

Their Faces Began to Glow

Even though I spend more than 5 percent of my life inside the walls of the church, do not think that means I always expect Jesus to show up there. I find myself reading and answering e-mails, sitting through seemingly endless committee meetings, pacing with families in the hospital waiting room during routine surgery, and staring for hours at the ceiling of my office wondering what in the world I am supposed to preach about on Sunday. I can easily get stuck in the daily routine and busyness for Jesus and as a result forget to keep an eye out for Jesus himself. But if I am mindful of his presences in the midst of the ordinary today, and a week from next Tuesday, Jesus often surprises me with the gift of joy.

On Wednesday mornings the children of our church's preschool gather in the sanctuary for chapel. It is always one of the highlights of my week to lead chapel, but on one particular week I was going through the motions. I had other things pressing on my mind. However, I did think I had crafted the perfect chapel talk. The lights in the sanctuary were off, giving the appearance of darkness even on a bright morning. I held up a mirror and asked the children to look into it. They claimed to be able to see themselves, though darkly. The kids in the fourth and fifth rows had a difficult time seeing anything. Next, I lit the large Christ candle in the chancel to remind the children that Christ is the light of the world. I had them look in the mirror again, and all of them said it was easier to see themselves with the light. A pretty clever illustration, I thought.

But the final step I had planned was the best. I asked the weekday school teachers to bring each child up to look closely in the mirror. As they came, I held the mirror behind the Christ candle so that they would see the flame flickering in their own face. I wanted them to see and know the light of Christ present in their lives. And so, one by one, they came to look at themselves in the mirror. I hoped it would be a memorable moment for each of them.

However, I did not expect what happened to me. In the darkness of the sanctuary, beginning with the four- and five-year-olds and moving to the threes and the twos, each child, one at a time, stepped up to the light. The eyes of each child were focused on the flickering flame and the reflection in the mirror. As I was holding the mirror, I could not see the children's faces in the glass. From my perspective, I could not even see the candle that was between the child and the mirror. All I could see was the face of each child. And as each child moved from the darkness into the light, I watched each face, full of wonder and amazement, literally begin to glow. And so did my heart. Christ's light filled each child's face. It was as if Christ himself was staring back at me. Joy overwhelmed me.

I thought it was an ordinary work day. I was going through the motions with too much on my mind. But Jesus surprised me by showing up where I work, and I knew joy.

Called to Go Where?

And so it is that we, even in the midst of our busy lives, continue to stumble upon joy a week from next Tuesday, in the mundane and ordinary events of daily living.

Often when we read the story of Jesus calling Simon and Andrew, James and John to follow him we stop with, "Immediately they left their nets and followed him." Yet, once as I was preparing to preach on Mark 1:14–20, a question ran through my mind. Perhaps this question came to me because, at the time, I was attending a class in Scotland and missed my family. Maybe I was bored with this familiar story or puzzled by the abruptness of its ending. But I wondered, "Where did Jesus take the disciples?" They left their nets and their work and their business lying there on the side of the Sea of Galilee to follow Jesus; but where did they go?

Would they go to a mountain retreat to meditate and reflect upon Scripture? Would they travel to a quiet garden to remain silent while listening to great teaching? Does Jesus invite them to a solitary life of prayer and worship? So for the first time, I intentionally read the next verse.

"They went to Capernaum," (Mark 1:21). Christ takes his first disciples to Capernaum. This is the city in which they lived. This is the location of the synagogue in which they worshipped. But if we keep reading this first chapter of Mark's Gospel, we find that Jesus did not take them to the synagogue, nor did he hide them away in some isolated retreat. Instead, he took them to Simon's house and interacted with Simon's family. Christ did not call these first disciples to follow him out of the relationships and ordinary activities that define their lives. No, Christ called them to follow him, and he led them back into the complicated and complex web of their world!

This news shocked me. Yet I quickly realized that going to Capernaum does not make the call to follow Christ any easier for his disciples. In fact, this path was probably more difficult, more demanding, and more radical. Imagine if you were called to give it all up, to go and sit day by day, one on one, at the foot of God. Who among us wouldn't say yes? Trade all our other relationships for an exclusive relationship with God? Sure. But, for us, to follow Christ means engaging in the everyday concerns and relationships of family and friends, church and churches, government and business, doctors and schools. To follow and know Christ means to constantly juggle all our other commitments and demands. To follow Christ means to see all our relationships in terms of how we follow Christ in this interaction, and that one, and the next. That is the challenge of saying "yes" when Jesus calls, "Follow me." And yet, these ordinary moments of life also present opportunities to see Christ and know the gift of joy, because Christ is present precisely in these ordinary moments.

As Jesus continues with his public ministry, we learn that the Christ who is present with us was not accustomed to a warm bed in the evening. He said, "Foxes have holes and birds of the air have nests; but the Son of Man has nowhere to lay his head" (Matt 8:20). The Lord who continues to be present with us fed the multitudes not with six months wages, but with a child's simple lunch of five loaves and two fish (John 6:1–14). As he teaches the crowds with parables, Jesus tells stories about a sower who sows his field, day laborers and a generous employer, a shepherd looking for lost sheep, and a woman sweeping for lost coins. Jesus goes to weddings and dinner parties; he visits in the homes of his friends, and he takes boat rides on the sea. Yes, a week from next Tuesday is where Jesus spent "his 95" from the beginning and throughout his ministry.

And so it naturally follows that it is in simple and incarnational ways that Christ surprises us with his presence and with joy.

Your life and mine are no less busy than the lives of Jesus' first disciples. However, even in the mundane ordinariness and busyness of life, Jesus keeps showing up. In fact, it is precisely in these moments that we might know joy. I have mentioned Alexander Schmemann to you in previous chapters of this book. Throughout his personal journals, Father Schmemann spends a great deal of time reflecting on the nature of joy. In one entry he writes: "Day after day—the same sun, the same happiness: the lake, the mountains, the greenery, the light. Nothing special happens. Mornings until lunch—work . . . After lunch, long walks with [my wife], every day a new one—an unending delight."[2] Yes, it is often in the simple delight of a day *in which nothing special happens* that Schmemann receives the gift of joy.

Can that be true for you and for me? While busyness can cloud our vision so that we cannot perceive Christ's presence with us, could it be that our busyness also provides us with multiple opportunities to notice Christ and know joy?

Caller ID

Very early in my ministry a friend sent me a *Kudzu* cartoon. The cartoon was undated and I do not know from which newspaper my friend had cut the strip. *Kudzu* was a daily comic strip by Doug Marlette and ran from 1981 to 2007 and ended when Marlette was tragically killed in a car accident. The strip centered on a small fictional North Carolina town called "Bypass." Two of the main characters were a sixteen-year-old young man named Kudzu Dubose and the town's minister whose name was Rev. Will B. Dunn.

The particular cartoon that was passed on to me had Kudzu and Rev. Dunn sitting together at the top of a hill, their backs to the reader. In the first frame, Kudzu, apparently staring into the distance, asks, "Preacher, how did you wind up in a place like Bypass?" The next frame has Rev. Dunn turning his head to look at the

2. Schmemann, *Journals*, 82.

young man. With a smile on his face he replies, "I was called." The final frame has Kudzu still staring out into the distance, and he says, "Don't you have Caller ID?"

I've kept that cartoon, now yellowed and partially torn, on my office desk ever since. I share it with you not only because I laugh out loud every time I read it, but because I am convinced that every moment of every day, we are exactly where God has placed us. And if God has placed you and me there, then Christ is with us there just as he promised. As we know Christ in that busy and ordinary moment we might receive the gift of joy.

As you reflect upon the moments in your life when you either notice or miss Christ's presence with you, I want you to imagine that today you receive a phone call from your bank. You verify that it really is your bank calling and not some scam. The person on the phone tells you that you have won a contest you did not know you had even entered. As the contest winner the bank is going to give you $86,400 every day. That is correct—$86,400 each and every day.

But there are a few rules, a few strings attached. Three in fact:

Rule number 1. You cannot move the money into another bank account. You can write as many checks on the account and spend as much of the money as you would like, but you cannot transfer the money to another bank.

Rule number 2. Whatever amount of the $86,400 that you do not spend in a single day, you will lose. You must spend it all. It is like manna in the wilderness that cannot be carried over to the next day. Any amount left in the account will not be there in the morning.

Rule number 3. Without any prior notice, at some point the bank will close the account and you will receive no more daily payments. The prize will end at the bank's discretion and there will be no more money.

So, you will receive $86,400 every day to spend and do with however you like, but you cannot move the money to another bank, any amount you do not spend in a day you will lose, and you never know when the contest will end.

Even with those conditions, what an amazing gift that would be. What would you do with that kind of money knowing that you had to use it each and every day? I am sure that all of you would tithe every day, right? But what about after that? What would you buy? Who would you help? What debts would you pay off? What gifts would you make? If you think about it, that amount of money would allow you to make a difference in this world; to change lives; to make things better for your family, your friends, for your community, for those in other parts of the world. So, what would you do with $86,400 dollars a day?

Well, God has given you and given me, 86,400 seconds every day. You can do the math, but that is the number of seconds in twenty-four hours. God has given those seconds to you and to me as a gift. We can't give our seconds to anyone else; we cannot roll the seconds over to another day—we must use them today or lose them forever; and we never know when our seconds will run out.

God has given us each of those seconds. From the time when the alarm first goes off until the moment we fall asleep in front of the television to the second the alarm goes off for another day, each second is a gift. And Christ is present with you in every one of those 86,400 seconds. Christ calls you to follow him, to know him, and to receive the gift of joy, in each and every one of those ordinary seconds today and a week from next Tuesday.

Finding Jesus at the Ballpark

For the last two springs and early summers, I have spent some of my 86,400 seconds every day coaching youth baseball. Despite the challenges of time and potentially overzealous parents, I agreed to coach because I love baseball and I love my children. Coaching allows me to join both of those loves. As a child and teen I always played baseball—from five years old through high school. My mother would play catch with me in the backyard until I started throwing too hard and hurt her hand. Then I had to wait for my dad to get home from work or convince the "big kids" who played in the field behind our house to let me in their game. Baseball is in my blood.

And I love my kids. My son Sam played on the Rangers. He played pitcher last year and shortstop this year. He has grown into a good all-around player and made the All Star team. It is fun to be his coach.

My older son Will has learned to keep score, marking singles, doubles, and outs, noting where each player on the other team hit the ball so I could better position my defense the next time through the order. He sat on the bench; he ran the scoreboard; and he proved himself to be an invaluable aide to me as coach.

My daughter Bekah loves to play baseball with her brothers in the backyard. She is becoming quite a little hitter herself. And she is convinced that when she starts playing T-ball that I'm going to coach her team too!

Yes, I love my children and I love baseball. That may be enough. But there is something more. In the midst of this ordinary activity of fathers and sons and daughters, Jesus showed up and I knew the gift of joy.

So because I coach baseball, I led the prayer at the Lumberton Youth Baseball Association Opening Day ceremonies with several hundred players, coaches, and parents in attendance.

Because I coach baseball, I am now friends with a Pentecostal youth pastor who was one of my assistant coaches. Both of our ministries are richer for our friendship.

Because I coach baseball, a child of First Presbyterian Church who moved back to Lumberton to practice law found a place to belong when so much about his hometown has changed.

Because I coach baseball, I prayed for a father in the hospital with seizures and for his worried wife, daughter, and son.

Because I coach baseball, I met Possum and the other amazingly supportive and positive parents of the Rangers.

Because I coach baseball, a father and a son who were disillusioned after last year's season grew to love the game again.

Because I coach baseball, I waited one evening after a game for an hour with a boy whose mother works second shift at a day care. She couldn't find anyone to come get him, but the boy and his mother knew someone was looking out for him that night.

Because I coach baseball, I came to know the tremendous hard work, long hours, and dedication of other coaches and league officials.

Because I coach baseball, parents of my team and other teams saw us pray before each game.

Because I coach baseball, I am and will always be at least a small part of the lives of the Rangers.

Because I coach baseball, I get the chance to glimpse Jesus and know joy in seconds.

"Hello, Monica? This is Matt Rich."

"Hey Matt, what's up? We don't play you in soccer today, do we?"

"No, actually I'm calling about baseball."

"Are you calling me with good news for Daniel?"

"Well, yes, Monica. I think I am."

Questions for Reflection

1. What might happen if you started expecting Jesus to be present every day at your work or at your home?

2. Share with someone a time when Jesus showed up in the midst of an ordinary or mundane moment in your life?

3. What would you do with $86,400 dollars to spend every day? How will you choose to spend your 86,400 seconds tomorrow?

4. What do you do just because you love it? Do you ever find Christ and the gift of joy in the midst of those moments?

5

With One Eye Squinted

Habakkuk 3:17–19; Luke 23:32–43;
and John 16:20–22

CANCER. MY COUSIN KRISTIE has cancer. She just turned thirty-nine years old and she has cancer. As I said earlier about tragedy, it only takes one. Kristie has cancer for the second time. Where is Christ in that? How can anyone find joy in this?

At the age of twenty-seven, Kristie discovered a lump in her breast. Tests and a biopsy confirmed cancer. She was young. She was otherwise healthy. She prayed. Her husband, Chad, prayed. Her friends and family all prayed and prayed and prayed. Kristie found some of the best treatment available for her type of cancer in her own hometown. Surgery, chemo, and radiation. She lost her long blond hair, but her body responded. We heard the good news: the cancer was gone! What a day of rejoicing that was!

In the eleven years since that blessed day, Kristie and Chad have lived full and busy lives. They were like many young Christian couples. They worked, went to graduate school, built and furnished a home or two. In their local church they worshipped, prayed, taught, served, and led. They witnessed to God's presence, grace, and care in the ordinary and extraordinary moments of life. I am sure you know plenty of people just like them in your church. They may even be like you.

Because Kristie's breast cancer had been estrogen based, the doctors told her that pregnancy could be dangerous to her health. So Kristie and Chad adopted two beautiful children—a girl Emilie, and then a boy, Daniel. The members of this family have grown and laughed and struggled. They are like any young family this way. In good days and bad days, they trust in the Lord for guidance and wisdom. Kristie and Chad know Christ, and they know joy.

Some hip and back pain sent Kristie back to the oncologist. Kristie told me that once you have had cancer, the thought of it coming back is always with you. The doctors ran tests. The tests confirmed her worries. The cancer was back. But this time it was in her bones. Where is Christ in that? How can there be joy?

In the previous chapter of this book I explored how even coaching youth baseball can be an opportunity to know Christ's presence and great joy! However, Christians know as well as anyone that life a week from next Tuesday might be filled with much more than afternoons drinking honeysuckle and evenings at the ballpark. Confusion, despair, illness, pain, suffering, and death all plague human life. In the midst of such tragedy how can Christians still know the surprising joy of Christ's presence?

With One Eye Squinted

Have you ever read the writings of the prophet Habakkuk, from the book in the Bible? If you have, did you read a sermon from this book? Probably not. Habakkuk is the eighth out of twelve Minor Prophets noted at the end of the Old Testament. While we do not know too much about this prophet, it seems that he spoke the word of the Lord in the days leading up to the destruction of Jerusalem and the deportation of the people of Israel into exile in Babylon. Imagine the first days of the financial crisis in 2008, plus knowing that you will lose your home next week and will have to move out of state, and you will get a sense of Habakkuk's context.

Yet it is in the midst of tragedy, uncertainty, and fear that Habakkuk speaks of the persistence of joy.

> Though the fig tree does not blossom,
> and no fruit is on the vines;
> though the produce of the olive fails
> and the fields yield no food;
> though the flock is cut off from the fold
> and there is no herd in the stalls,
> yet I will rejoice in the Lord;
> I will exult in the God of my salvation
> God, the Lord, is my strength;
> He makes my feet like the feet of a deer
> and he makes me tread upon the heights. (Hab 3:17–19)

Famine and starvation threatened his people. The nation faced a dreadful harvest and the loss of livestock. For the prophet, there is nothing in Israel's work or circumstances that call for levity or amusement. Any pursuit of happiness through one's own labor has proven futile. It appears that tragedy prevails. And yet, still the prophet claims, "I will rejoice in the Lord." Notice that, just as it was for Paul in his letter to the Philippians, Israel's rejoicing is *in the Lord* for *God, the Lord* is his salvation and strength. Even in the midst of tragedy, God's faithful presence remains and can be perceived.

The letters of the great southern American author Flannery O'Connor reflect a similar sense of God's presence in the face of tragic circumstances. O'Connor was only twenty-five years old when doctors diagnosed her with lupus, a disease in which the body attacks itself and its organs as if they were intruders. Drained of much of her energy and stamina, O'Connor returned to her mother's farm where she began raising peacocks and exotic birds and continued to write. Although essentially confined to her home, she maintained friendships and correspondence with many in the literary world through volumes of letters. In one letter composed shortly after moving back home, O'Connor writes:

> I am making out fine in spite of any conflicting stories. I
> have a disease called lupus and I take a medicine called
> ACTH and I manage well enough to live with both.
> Lupus is one of those things in the rheumatic depart-
> ment; it comes and goes, when it comes I retire and when

it goes, I venture forth. My father had it some twelve or fifteen years ago but at that time there was nothing for it but the undertaker; now it can be controlled with the ACTH. I have enough energy to write with and as that is all I have any business doing anyhow, I can with one eye squinted take it all as a blessing.[1]

To be essentially confined to her home as a young adult, especially after living and traveling throughout the United States in pursuit of her writing, was a tragedy for O'Connor. Her disease and its unpredictable drains upon her energy and ability to write would prove immensely frustrating to the young author. Yet, still she was able to recognize the presence of God in it all. She knew that God had called her to be a writer, and she had energy enough for that, so she was able "with one eye squinted [to] take it all as a blessing." Yes, O'Connor knew joy even in the midst of most difficult circumstances.

With a Kiss

I find Flannery O'Connor's story a helpful reminder because often "one eye squinted" is all we get. When I was in seminary, I spent a summer at Baptist Hospital in Winston-Salem working as a student chaplain. It was a challenging experience for me because on a daily basis I found myself attempting to bring God's presence, light, and word into life and death situations.

Three times over the summer, I served as the chaplain "on call" overnight at the hospital, the only chaplain in the hospital during those hours. My first night, even before it was really night, I received a call from the ICU because a young man was dying.

As I entered the unit, there was chaos in the hallway. I quickly learned that the young man came from a broken and highly dysfunctional family. Mother and stepmother were yelling at one another. Aunts and sisters were crying in the hallway. Father and brothers were making threats against friends. Security was present,

1. O'Connor, "To Elizabeth and Robert Lowell," 57.

and I attempted to help calm everyone down and find their own
separate corners to allow them to work through their grief.

The young man, about twenty years old, had been shot in a
drive-by shooting. The incident was probably drug and gang related, which added to the tension. First he had been taken to another
hospital that stabilized him. That hospital sent him to Baptist for
critical care. Each time I saw him in the ICU, entering his room
accompanied by a few family members at a time, the tears began
to fall. He was hardly recognizable because his body had swelled
from all the fluid the medical staff had given him to maintain his
blood pressure. Tears fell from every family member as they saw
him. Together we prayed and we prayed.

After he had taken his last breath, and the chaos of grief and
anger and loss threatened to rage again in the hall outside, I found
myself in the room as one young female cousin, not older than 15,
remained by the young man's side. The decibels rose outside the
door, but she sat silently. Then quietly she stood, she bent over her
cousin, stretching to the full extent her body would allow, and gave
him a kiss on the forehead. Then she turned and walked out.

It was in that ordinary, silent, simple kiss that I glimpsed the
kingdom of heaven draw near. Christ was close enough to touch in
the midst of the darkness that raged outside. Yes, in that moment
Christ was there and, with one eye squinted, so was joy.

One on His Right and One on His Left

Even today, after writing about that experience in the ICU, I have
to take a moment to pause and dry my tears. Christ was there and
so was joy. I am convinced that we find Christ in the middle of
tragic experiences because Jesus had been right there in his own
life—on the cross. Perhaps we can see joy if we look at the account
of Christ's crucifixion in the Gospel of Luke with one eye squinted
(Luke 23:33–42).

Luke begins his narration of the crucifixion with the remark-
able brevity of a single verse: "When they came to the place that is
called The Skull, they crucified Jesus there with the criminals, one

on his right and one on his left." In addition to the two who also hung, arms outstretched, above the ground, a crowd had gathered. Some cast lots for his clothing, some just stood and stared. Luke reports that it was the leaders who first scoffed at Jesus, not realizing the truth of the words they shouted, "He saved others, let him save himself if he is the Messiah of God, his chosen one!" Soldiers offered Jesus sour wine and added to the irony of the moment by declaring, "If you are the King of the Jews, save yourself!" Even one of the criminals hanging on a cross beside him gets in on the act. "Are you not the Messiah? Save yourself and us!" And just in case we, as readers, have not yet caught on, an inscription rested above Jesus' head says, "This is the King of the Jews."

But this is not the king for whom we, nor the disciples for that matter, are looking. During Advent and Christmas we read texts from the prophet Isaiah that promise "the yoke of their burden and the bar across their shoulders, the rod of their oppressor, you have broken as on the day of Midian" (Isa 9:4) and "See the Lord God comes with might, and his arm rules for him" (Isa 40:10a). Even in Luke's own gospel we hear the opening verses of Mary's song of celebration: "Blessed be the Lord God of Israel, for he has looked favorably on his people and redeemed them. He has raised up a mighty savior for us in the house of his servant David" (Luke 2:68–69). A mighty savior with a strong arm, an arm so strong that breaks the rod of the oppressor—isn't that what we desire in a king? By the time of Jesus' crucifixion, the people of Palestine had grown tired of foreign rulers in general and of the cruel violence of their Roman occupiers in particular. A mighty savior sounded like a great idea to them. But what did they find, what do we find: a man betrayed, arrested, denied, mocked, beaten, and now crucified. The King of the Jews? Who wouldn't scoff and laugh at that?

But then, in a surprising development, the second criminal hanging beside Jesus rebukes the first criminal: "Do you not fear God, since you are under the same sentence of condemnation? And we indeed have been condemned justly, for we are getting what we deserve for our deeds, but this man has done nothing wrong." Somehow able to see through the pain, torture, noise, and commotion of the moment, this criminal accepts his punishment as justly deserved and recognizes that Jesus has done nothing to validate his place on a cross. For the first time in Luke's account of this tragic day, one person *recognizes* Jesus and knowingly speaks words of truth. If this one person truly sees Jesus, could he also know joy?

The second criminal calls Jesus by name, "Jesus, remember me when you come into your kingdom." This is not a statement of repentance. This is not a request for immediate deliverance. This is not a pledge to work harder and live better if given another chance. No, the criminal utters an expression of hope that this end is not the end. This is a statement of faith that, even in the midst of death, there is a kingdom yet to come. "Jesus, remember me when you come into your kingdom."

But what if this one criminal, a person who seems to see with such clarity, also has not fully realized the truth of what this moment holds? In Mark's Gospel, as Jesus and the disciples are on the road to Jerusalem, James and John ask Jesus if they can sit on his right and on his left in glory. Jesus responds, "To sit at my right hand or at my left is not mine to grant, but it is for those for whom it has been prepared" (Mark 10:40). As Jesus hangs on the cross, we find one on his right and one on his left. This is the moment in which God finally reveals Jesus' glory and purpose and Lordship over sin and death. In this moment of coronation, the places are filled: there is one hanging on his right and one hanging on his left. A crucified king with sinners taking the places of honor. Could it be that the kingdom is not to come, but is fully revealed by a man betrayed, arrested, denied, mocked, beaten, and now crucified?

So it is as king that Jesus, in this moment of glory and pain, responds to the second criminal, "Truly I tell you, today you will be with me in paradise." Not tomorrow, not sometime soon, not after a thousand years of penance, no, *today* you will be with me in paradise. Today—right here in this place called The Skull, with spikes in our hands and crowds deriding us, while soldiers give us sour wine to drink and we struggle to catch one last breath—today you will be with me in paradise.

With a king like that, paradise and joy do not have to be some pie-in-the-sky dream of a future where suffering and pain are no more. No, paradise and joy are wherever and whenever we are "with him," with the one who takes our suffering and pain upon himself, with the one who bears our sins and the sins of the world upon his back, with the one who hangs on a cross in a place called The Skull. With a king like that even a cross can be a throne. Whenever we notice a king like that, there we know joy.

No One Will Take Your Joy

When we, as Christians, view a tragic world with "one eye squinted" what we finally see will always be the cross of Christ. In the Eastern Orthodox liturgy for Sunday worship, there is a phrase that proclaims, "For through the Cross, joy came into the whole world." [2] Such an odd phrase for us today, that joy might come into the world through a cross. But it is precisely through the cross that Christ stands "with us" in the midst of the suffering, trials, and tribulations of life. Christ is the shoulder upon which we weep in our darkest moments. And through the cross even in our weeping we might find a clear and invincible joyfulness.

Yet there is more. Through the cross, Christ also gathers up all of humanity in himself—our sin, suffering, trials, tribulations and everything else—and carries them to God. All that we are, Christ has been and so we are united with him in both death and resurrection. Without death there can be no resurrection. As we will see in the next chapter, the victory of resurrection is a moment of joy that comes out from despair but does not avoid it. So to squint one eye and see the cross of Christ is to acknowledge our confusion, despair, pain, suffering, and death, but to know that in Christ even our greatest tragedies are moments in which we might know joy.

Thus, it is in the context of his impending death on the cross that Jesus speaks of the joy that cannot be taken from his disciples:

> Very truly I tell you, you will weep and mourn, but the world will rejoice; you will have pain, but your pain will turn into joy. When a woman is in labor, she has pain, because her hour has come. But when her child is born, she no longer remembers the anguish because of the joy

2. Schmemann, *For the Life*, 55.

of having brought a human being into the world. So you have pain now; but I will see you again, and your hearts will rejoice, and no one will take your joy from you (John 16:20–22).

The joy that is rightfully ours as Christians is a joy that is not immune to confusion, despair, pain, suffering, and death. Through the cross we know a joy in Christ that does not seek to avoid or escape the tragedies of life. Through the cross we know that even in the midst of the darkest night, light still shines and in God's loving care all will be well. Through the cross we know a joy that acknowledges the pain and difficulty of life, but transforms them through faith, hope, and love. Through the cross we know that the final word belongs not to death, but to Christ who has promised to see us again and who brings with him the joy of new life.

A Triple for Emilie

On the two year anniversary of her rediagnosis, a Wednesday, my cousin Kristie went to her cancer center to learn the results of her latest scans and tests. She and Chad heard easy news. No disease progression and perhaps even improvement in her bones; her tumor markers clearly in a "normal range." Treatment would continue with daily chemo pills, which to that point had very little impact on her day-to-day life. Today, she has energy. She still wears her blond hair in a ponytail. By all outward appearance she looks "normal."

Certainly great news! Circumstances that call for happiness, for sure.

And yet, on the day Kristie heard that easy news, she did not find joy in her prognosis. On that day, she found joy elsewhere.

That afternoon her daughter Emilie hit a triple in a softball game.

When your body is fighting cancer, your daughter hitting a triple in a 10U softball game might not sound like the most important news of the day. But it is. It is vitally important news when your daughter does not believe that she is very good at softball. And it is reassuring news when your daughter struggles with the fact that her parents committed her to playing the sport. It is great news because your daughter has wanted to quit softball from the first day she made the travel team. This news is a relief because your daughter bats at the end of the order, and your daughter hates batting because the whole world watches just her. This is joyful news because your daughter finds softball to be something that is only hard; that is only in her life because she cannot convince her parents to let her quit; because it is something that she wants to be done with yesterday; something she cannot imagine doing a week from next Tuesday.

But on that same Wednesday night, Emilie who is a sweet, unbelievably talented athlete who sometimes lets fear win and does not fully believe in the gift she has received, hit a triple. On that Wednesday night Emilie got a taste of the excitement that swells in your heart and causes your adrenaline to pulse through your body when you swing hard and feel the bat impact the ball just right. Emilie got a taste of what it is like to run around the bases, rounding second and taking a risk to head for third even though the throw is coming and you just might be out.

On that Wednesday night, Emilie got to stand on third, breathing hard, and experience the bliss of getting a high-five from her coach. Emilie got to hear the screams from the fans, including her mother making a fool out of herself in the stands. Emile saw the smiles on her teammates' faces and the two runs added to the scoreboard.

And in that moment, Kristie knew joy. Not because Emilie hit a triple, but because in that moment Christ revealed himself to her. Kristie realized that she often saw the hard part of her life—the cancer part—as something that she did only because she had to. Cancer is hard. It tempts her to fear. It requires all the strength she has, and way more that she doesn't have, in order to walk through it. She did not expect joy to come from it. Growth, sure. Redemption, absolutely. Coaching from Christ, the one and only coach we have, definitely. But not joy—in it, through it, because of it.

A bona fide triple to the outfield in a 10U softball game showed Kristie that she was wrong. She had been shortchanging God. Kristie writes:

It's funny to me how God reveals Himself to me. You would think that it would only come at times when I walk into [the cancer center] or when I am deep in prayer or when I am spending my time in the morning reading my Bible. Who knew that, after I made a fool of myself by cheering for my daughter like a crazed parent, God would be so kind to me and whisper a new truth in my ear:

I will bring you such joy from this hard thing. The very thing that you see as something you would stop in a heart-beat if I released you from it can—and will—bring YOU joy. Wait for it, Kristie. I will do it. And I will be cheer-ing for you and rejoicing over you and loving you all the while.[3]

We live in a world filled with tragedy, suffering, and pain. Yet, with one eye squinted, we might see the cross of Christ and know that while we have pain now, we will see Christ again. We never know when Christ will show up, but when he does arrive our hearts will rejoice and no one will take our joy from us. Not today. Not even a week from next Tuesday.

Questions for Reflection

1. In the midst of the world's tragedy and suffering, what is the "one" thing that leads to you ask, "Why?"

2. What would it be like to go through an entire day with one eye squinted so that you can take everything as blessing?

3. Try to imagine yourself at the crucifixion of Jesus? What do you see and feel? Could you describe that moment as "joy" or "paradise"?

4. Has God ever whispered in your ear in the midst of something incredibly hard? What did you hear? How did you experience joy in that moment?

3. Rush, "Update #37," para. 23.

6

The Comedy of Resurrection

*John 20:1–23; Luke 24:13–35;
and John 21:1–8*

DOES YOUR CHURCH CELEBRATE "Hilarity Sunday"? I recently learned of this ancient and yet strange tradition that comes to us from the Eastern Orthodox Church.[1] Each year, the Sunday after Easter is set aside as a day of hilarity. On that day, the venerable priests, wearing full Orthodox robes and vestments, with a congregation of worshippers sitting or standing before them, rise into the pulpit and begin telling jokes. The jokes they tell are not necessarily always religious. Rather, they are jokes just designed to elicit laughter from the congregation. Can you imagine laughter echoing off the old walls of an Orthodox church—a place steeped in tradition, candles, and incense? The pews shaking a little as worshippers hold their sides? The looks from passersby in the street who wonder at the joyful sounds the sanctuary cannot contain?

We have just finished a chapter about cancer, lupus, death, and crucifixion. Christ is present in the midst of those most challenging situations, of course. But such episodes still threaten to overwhelm us. The world and the church demand serious answers to problems like these. There is no time for jokes.

Well, maybe just one:

---

1. Copenhaver, "Laughter at Easter," 15.

> Did you know that the plans God gave Noah to build the ark called for three stories? The top story had a window to let light in, but how did light get to the bottom two stories? Floodlights.

That's enough of that, right? I am a Presbyterian pastor, and they do not call Presbyterians the "frozen-chosen" for nothing. Well, maybe just one more:

> There once was a mother tomato walking with her baby tomato. The young tomato kept falling behind. The mother would stop and wait before going on. Finally, as the young tomato fell back once again, the mother tomato stopped, stepped on the baby tomato and said, "Catch-up!"

I do not think I should stop there. There must be a better joke than a tomato joke!

> One day after church the pastor was shaking hands. He saw a man he hadn't seen in a while, so he pulled him aside and said, "Sir, you need to join the Army of the Lord!"
>
> The man replied, "I'm already in the Army of the Lord, pastor."
>
> The minister asked, "Then why is it that I only see you on Christmas and Easter?"
>
> The man pulled the pastor close, and whispered, "Because I'm in the secret service."

If you too are in the secret service, you must have a lot of questions for God.

> One day a man was praying and he decided to ask God some important questions:
>
> He said, "God, is it true that a thousand years are like a second to you?
>
> God responded: "Yes, that's true."
>
> The man asked, "Well then, God, how much is a million dollars to you?"
>
> God responded again: "It's like a penny."
>
> The man said, "God could you give me penny."

God said, "Sure, it will just take a second."

Speaking of money . . .

> There were three boys arguing on the playground one day about whose father was the best.
> The first boy says, "My Dad scribbles a few words on a piece of paper, he calls it a poem, they give him $50."
> The second boy says, "That's nothing. My Dad scribbles a few words on a piece of paper, he calls it a song, and they give him $100."
> The third boy says, "I got you both beat. My Dad scribbles a few words on a piece of paper, he calls it a sermon . . . and it takes eight people to collect all the money!"

Then there is the favorite joke of my childhood . . .

> Two men jump out of an airplane from 10,000 feet. They fell through the air for a while until they got to 5,000 feet. The one pulled his parachute and it opened, but the other man kept falling. His friend called to him and said, "You need to pull your chute!" His friend replied: "Nah."
> The man fell to about 1,000 feet and his friend said, "Pull your chute!" "Nah," the reply came back.
> As the man fell to about 300 feet, his friend began to get worried. "Pull your chute!" "Nah."
> The man continued to fall; he was about fifty feet from the ground. In his ear, he heard his friend, "It's almost too late! Pull your chute! "Nah."
> Finally, he was about 10 feet from the ground. His friend yelled: "It's your last chance! Pull your chute!"
> The man replied, "Nah, I can jump from here."

Would it shock you to know that I told all of those jokes in church? Now, it may come as a surprise to you that Presbyterians can laugh a little. It may be a reversal of your expectations. In chapters three and four of this book we saw the surprising element of joy as we stumble upon Christ in the ordinary events of daily life. Could it be that in moments of tragedy and suffering, we might also be surprised by joy? Even when we initially miss Jesus through our tears, might he appear to us as a gift resulting in amazement, wonder, and even laughter? Yes. That is what resurrection is all about.

My Holy Week

Holy Week—the week between Palm Sunday and Easter—is usually a very busy week for me as a pastor. Holy Week bubbles with emotion, worship, community, and Scripture. Despite its many demands, this is one of my favorite weeks of the year to be a pastor. However, a few years ago I experienced a most unusual Holy Week.

On Palm Sunday—immediately after our moving worship services that included singing, special music, and time to reflect upon Jesus' arrest, death, and burial—my dad, my mom, Sarah, Will, Sam, Bekah, and I all piled into our minivan and began a trip to Buffalo, New York. Because of this family trip, I missed the youth presentation that I had really been looking forward to seeing. The presentation, scheduled for Sunday evening, was a Stations of the Cross experience called *In the Footsteps of Jesus*. But, we were not going to Buffalo that Sunday afternoon for a vacation. We were going for the funeral of my grandmother. Gram had died two days before. She was ninety-three years old, almost ninety-four. So, with seven of us in the car, we drove halfway to Buffalo on Sunday and the other half on Monday.

As members of our church concluded a noon service on Monday at the neighboring Methodist congregation, my family and I emerged from lunch in Meadsville, Pennsylvania, to find that it had started to rain. The date was April 18. In Lumberton that day, it was almost 80 degrees. In Pennsylvania it was 41 degrees. As we drove north into New York State, the temperature dropped and the rain turned into snow. By the time we arrived at the hotel in Buffalo, it was snowing hard, gathering lightly on the grass and trees, but luckily not sticking to the road. An unusual start to Holy Week.

On Tuesday, we gathered first at the mausoleum for Gram's committal service, which I led. After lunch as a family, we gathered at the Eden United Methodist Church for a memorial service. So instead of preaching for the noon Holy Week service in Lumberton at First Presbyterian, I preached at my grandmother's funeral. No, not a typical Holy Week at all.

On Wednesday, we, all seven of us in the minivan, drove all the way home to Lumberton. With a few short stops, it was a thirteen and a half hour trip. That is a long time to be in the car together. I missed the noon Holy Week service at First Baptist that day, and I did not return home in time to finish a Wednesday night Bible study series I was leading on Jesus' parables in Jerusalem. Even though our church had spent the seven weeks before Easter exploring Jesus' final week in Jerusalem, I still felt like I was somehow missing Holy Week.

Thursday I was back at the church playing catch up: a bulletin for Easter Sunday to finish, an evening worship service to prepare, and a noon service at Godwin Heights Baptist to attend. That afternoon, I also had my first chance to visit with members of our church who had suffered damage from tornados that swept through Lumberton on the Saturday before Palm Sunday. That had lain heavy on my heart all week as well. Our community and our church members had suffered from those tornados, and I was not in town to be present with them. When I walked through the door of one home, after seeing the yard and the house in various stages of cleanup and repair, all I could do was give the owner a hug. No words, just a hug.

Friday, as the rains came, I found myself still trying to catch up and prepare for Easter Sunday. I went to Trinity Episcopal for the final noon service of the week. Once again I heard the story of Jesus' arrest, trial, death, and burial and watched as members of that church carried a large cross into the sanctuary. The many ways that I had fallen short, so many plans for this week left undone, hit me as that service came to a close. An unexpected afternoon visit to the hospital for a pastoral call brought home to me once again how Holy Week had not gone according to plan, both my plan and other's plans too.

Saturday was a good day, with an Easter egg hunt for the kids at my mom and dad's and an uneventful trip to take care of a few errands. But on the way home we drove through one of the neighborhoods damaged by the tornados. While the cleanup was underway, the downed trees, damaged homes, and work left to be done settled heavy upon my heart. Then that night, after getting the kids to bed, as I worked on my Easter Sunday sermon, I got an e-mail asking for urgent prayer as a friend's son was having seizures that doctors were unable to control.

That was my "Holy Week." And that is what I brought with me to the tomb on that Easter Sunday. I brought with me death and destruction, failure and shortcomings, so many things out of my control, and the stress and fatigue that accompany it all. Yes, that is what I brought with me to the tomb that Easter morning. In the face of the overwhelming tragedy, suffering, and pain in the world and even your own life, perhaps you bring something like this to the tomb as well.

Where Easter Begins

I share with you the story of my Holy Week because Easter begins with tears, pain, tragedy, and loss. Inviting us to enter the Gospel of John's Easter morning account (John 20:1–23), biblical scholar Tom Wright suggests: "Stand with [Mary] as she weeps. Think of someone you know, or have seen on television or in the newspapers, who has cried bitterly this last week. Bring them too, and stand there with Mary. Don't rush it. Tears have their own natural rhythm. Hold them—the people, the tears—in your mind as you stand outside the tomb. And then when the moment is right, stoop down and look into the tomb itself."[2]

After the events of Good Friday, the morning of the third day held all the markings of a tragedy. The hero of the story lies dead, wrapped in cloth, in a tomb, behind a large stone. Those who followed him had scattered. Even the initial events of the morning indicate loss. "Early on the first day of the week, while it was still dark, Mary Magdalene came to the tomb and saw that the stone had been removed." Her first thought is not resurrection, but theft. She runs to tell the disciples, "They have taken the Lord out of the tomb and we do not know where they have laid him."

After returning to the tomb with Peter and the disciple Jesus loved, Mary is overcome with despair. As she stoops down to look into the tomb the sight of angels surprises her. Where in the world

2. Wright, *John for Everyone,"* 145.

did those angels come from? They were not there the first time Mary looked into the tomb. They were not there when Peter and the disciple whom Jesus loved walked right into that tomb. But there they are. Do you think that the angels can only be glimpsed through tears? Perhaps.

When angels show up in Scripture they tell us not to be afraid. When people are in tears, angels ask them why they are crying. We need to speak our fears, our loss, and our pain aloud. We need to say it and hear it. Just as Mary lamented that first Easter morning, "They have taken away . . ." you and I can fill in the blank today. They had taken away my Holy Week, my grandmother, and my control. Listen to your own voice and to the voices of those whom you bring with you to the tomb. They have taken away my home, my husband, my wife, my children, my health, my independence, my rights, my dignity, my hope. They have taken away my master. "They have taken away my Lord."

In that confession, in that admission of loss and pain and grief, our hearts turn with Mary's and we see a strange figure standing there. Yes, tragedy so often clouds our ability to see clearly. Who is he? What is he doing? And why does he know our names?

It is only in the presence of the risen Lord, who at first she mistakes for the gardener, that Mary knows joy. It is this surprising encounter with the risen Christ that changes Mary's tune so that she goes and joyfully announces to the disciples, "I have seen the Lord!" This is the fulfillment of the promise Jesus makes to his disciples in John 16. He promised that when they saw him again they would know joy. On Easter morning they saw him resurrected. They knew joy. Behold the risen Christ.

That is Easter. That is resurrection. The Lord stands right beside the tomb and calls us by name. In the midst of all that we have lost, in all the ways we have fallen short, through our very tears, the Lord stands right beside the tomb and calls us by name. And in that moment our eyes are opened and we can declare with Mary, "I have seen the Lord!"

A Mockery of Death

We have to admit that in the midst of a story with all the markings of a tragedy, resurrection is a surprising, might we even say comic, development. Admit what you will, but it is definitely a reversal of expectations. Despite the fact that Jesus had told them, multiple times, of his return, *no one* in the story anticipates resurrection. On Good Friday it appears that tragedy and death will have the final word. Three days later, the women arrive at the tomb expecting to anoint a corpse. And yet, when the women arrive they find the stone rolled away, the tomb empty, the body gone, and messengers telling them: "He is risen!" Through Christ's resurrection, concepts like liberation, freedom, and laughter suddenly become possible in a world of sin and death. The world is changed, death is no longer the final answer, and our perception of joy is irrevocably altered. As Protestant reformer Martin Luther wrote, "Through Christ's death and by virtue of his resurrection, 'death has become a mockery.'"[3]

Thus, Mary runs to the disciples and declares, "I have seen the Lord!" Not alone in her joy, later that evening Jesus comes and stands among the disciples as they have gathered in a locked room. In his presence, as they see him again, the disciples' fear is transformed into joy, for "then the disciples rejoiced when they saw the Lord."

Other resurrection encounters with the disciples are marked by similar surprising, almost comic, transformations from despair to joy. On resurrection day, two disciples travel to the village of Emmaus (Luke 24:13–35). The actual location of the town of Emmaus has been lost to history, but I think we all know the way. Presbyterian minister and writer, Frederick Buechner, has said that Emmaus could be:

> A bar, a night club, a movie, the place where we throw up our hands and say "Let the whole thing be hanged. It makes no difference anyway" . . . Emmaus may be buying some new clothes or a new car, smoking or drinking too much. Emmaus may even be going to church. Emmaus is whatever we do or wherever we go to make ourselves

3. Moltmann, *Theology and Joy*, 51.

forget that the world holds nothing sacred: that even
the wisest and bravest and loveliest decay and die, that
even the noblest ideas that [people] have—ideas about
love and freedom and justice—have always in time been
twisted out of shape by selfish men for selfish ends.[4]

On their journey, these two disciples are forced to explain the
reality and tragedy of death to a stranger who unexpectedly joins
them and seemingly knows nothing of the events that have taken
place in Jerusalem. Even though their eyes are clouded by the tragic
events of the last three days, as they walk their hearts burn within
them as the stranger opens the Scriptures to them. They finally
recognize their companion as the risen Christ in the breaking of
bread. Barely able to contain their joy, they run back to Jerusalem
to announce this good news.

Consider also the final story in the Gospel of John as Simon
Peter and the other disciples go fishing (John 21:1–8). At the end
of a long night, with empty boats, the disciples see a stranger on
the shore. This stranger tells them to "Cast the net to the right side
of the boat" and they will find some fish. Doing so results in such
a great catch that "they were not able to haul it in because there
were so many fish." In the midst of such abundance, the disciple
whom Jesus loved said to Peter, "It is the Lord!" Overcome by joy
in Christ's presence, Peter "puts on his clothes," jumps into the sea,
and swims the hundred yards to the shore. A more comic and joyful
scene it is hard to imagine.

Thus, in the face of certain tragedy, suffering, pain, and even
death, resurrection is a surprising and even comic facet to joy in
Christ. I believe that part of the reason we fail to perceive joy in
the church today is that, somewhere along the way, probably in our
attempts to be faithful to Christ's call of utmost importance, we've
forgotten that the news we Christians have is "gospel," *good news*.
We have forgotten that, as the church, we know the joy of resurrection. As Tom Currie writes: "Such joy, while not a mood, is a gift
that issues in a certain boldness of spirit, a kind of unapologetic
delight in the beauty and truth of Easter, which soon takes the form

4. Buechner, *The Magnificent Defeat*, 85–86.

of 'proclaiming the kingdom of God and teaching about the Lord Jesus Christ with all boldness [*parrhesias*, boldly, joyfully] and unhindered'" (Acts 28:31).[5]

A Christian Comedian

There are not many mainstream television shows that portray this kind of joy-filled Christian faith with integrity. So to be honest, I was surprised when a few years ago I stumbled upon *Studio 60 on the Sunset Strip*, an NBC show that unfortunately has been canceled. During its brief one season run, *Studio 60* attempted to depict the drama behind the scenes of a late night comedy sketch show. One of the characters on the show is a woman named Harriet Hayes. This character is a gifted comedian who is also a devout Christian. She maintains an on-again, off-again romantic relationship with another character, executive producer and head writer Matt Albie. On one episode, in an attempt to explain her Christian faith to a skeptical Matt, Harriet shares the story of her conversion at the age of eleven. She says:

"My mother put me in church plays and one time I just [totally forgot my line] and to cover I went into a Judy Holliday impression. There was stunned silence until the minister burst out laughing, and I looked and I saw the pride on my mother's face, and I told her I was ready to accept Christ and I was baptized."

Matt responds, "So are you saying that you became a Christian and a comedian at the same time?"

To which Harriet says, "I guess so."[6]

Who would have thought that Hollywood could have it exactly right? To be a Christian is to know joy; to be a Christian is to be a comedian in the face of the world's tragedy, knowing that the joke is not on us. As the man who refused to pull his parachute might say, all it takes is a change in perspective. Suffering, pain, and death will not laugh last. They are trumped by joy, which came to the whole world through a cross. The tomb stands empty! Jesus

5. Currie, *Joy of Ministry*, 4.
6. "Long Lead Story," *Studio 60*, NBC television.

is on the loose, and even in the midst of suffering and tragedy he shows up calling us by name. This is good news of great joy, so let us "Rejoice in the Lord always; again I will say, Rejoice!" (Phil 4:4).

I Saw the Lord

If I was going to share the entire story of my unusual Holy Week, then I could share a bit more with you.

I would tell you that I saw the Lord just after we got on the interstate on Sunday night when we passed a tour bus beside the road with the back end completely burned out and no one injured.

I saw the Lord on Monday and Tuesday as twenty-nine out of thirty members of my immediate family gathered with extended family and friends with joy and thanksgiving, even amid our tears, to truly celebrate my grandmother's life.

I saw the Lord on Wednesday as we spent thirteen and half hours in the car together. Despite the fact that my daughter threw up all over herself and her car seat about half way home, it still turned out to be one of the smoothest and most uneventful car trips I have ever taken with my family.

I saw the Lord when friends, congregation members, and colleagues led services and Bible studies in my absence.

I saw the Lord on Thursday afternoon when members of our church worked to repair homes damaged by the tornados and brought hope in the midst of despair.

I saw the Lord in hugs given and received among my colleagues in ministry following the Maundy Thursday evening service we hosted.

I saw the Lord on Friday and Saturday as healing and recovery began.

I saw the Lord on Sunday morning in each member and visitor who gathered for worship that Easter Sunday.

Yes, it had been an unexpected and yet most holy and joyful week for me. For I saw the Lord and he is risen indeed!

Questions for Reflection

1. What is your favorite joke? Tell your favorite joke to at least three people today.

2. What do you normally experience during Holy Week? Do you typically know joy during the week between Palm Sunday and Easter?

3. Have you ever glimpsed Christ or angels through your tears? How did you find joy in that moment?

4. So many comedians today rely upon irony or sarcasm for laughs. Is it possible to be a Christian and a comedian at the same time? Why or why not?

5. How does Christ's resurrection enable you to know joy in the midst of the tragedy, suffering, pain, and death you experience in your own life?

7

The Joyful Feast

*Luke 15:1–32; Luke 24:36–53;
and John 21:1–14*

GOD FIRST CALLED ME, upon graduation from seminary, to serve as pastor of the Salem/Pageland Presbyterian Church in Pageland, South Carolina. The saints of Pageland loved Sarah and me. They forgave my early mistakes in ministry and taught me much about being a pastor. The church itself was a small, traditional congregation in a small, traditional southern town. With a worship attendance of approximately seventy-five faithful souls on a strong Sunday, finding four new elders each year to serve on the church governing board, the Session, sometimes presented a problem.

One year the nominating committee approached a long-time member of the church to see if she would be willing to have her name placed in nomination. The entire congregation greatly respected both her and her husband. Her husband had served on the Session several times. However, this was the first time she had ever been asked. She told the committee she would pray about it.

A few days later she came by the church office. For thirty minutes or so, we talked about the responsibilities of being an elder, the typical operating procedures of the church, and the ways her particular gifts would be helpful to the church at that time. Toward the end of the conversation she said, "Matt, I really think God is calling me to do this, but my biggest problem is that I don't have a black suit."

I was quite perplexed, and I asked her what she meant. She replied, "You know the elders serve communion and I can't possibly serve communion unless I have a black suit!"

I told her not to worry because elders could wear whatever color they wanted when serving communion, even bright red. She laughed and our conversation came to an end. A few months later, the first time this new elder served communion, she was wearing her new black suit and a bright red scarf.

Where's the Beef?

Do you remember the "Where's the Beef?" television commercials?[1] The first of these commercials, which started airing in 1984, featured three older women, all wearing black dresses like they were getting ready for communion, gathered around a hamburger bun. After commenting on how large the bun was, they removed the top of the bun to reveal a tiny hamburger patty. One of the women looked at the hamburger and asked, "Where's the beef?" Although the commercial was designed to highlight the larger hamburgers at the chain Wendy's, the catchphrase quickly outgrew the ad itself and took on a life of its own.

Now I may be a bit odd, but when I read the Gospel of Luke's account of Jesus appearing to the disciples in Jerusalem on the night of his resurrection I think of that commercial. In the last chapter of this book we looked briefly at the resurrected, but mysterious, Jesus joining two disciples as they walked to Emmaus. When they reach their destination, Jesus tries to go on, but the disciples insist that he stay and eat with them. Jesus does so, and in the breaking of bread the disciples' eyes are opened and they recognized him. Yet as they do, Jesus disappears. Immediately the two disciples run back to Jerusalem with great joy to tell the other disciples about their encounter with the resurrected Lord.

While the disciples are talking about all this, Jesus himself appears among them declaring, "Peace be with you" (Luke 24:36). This terrifies some of the disciples, but Jesus reassures them and

1. *Where's the Beef?*, no page.

shows them his hands and his feet. Then in a fascinating verse, Luke reports the disciples' response: "In their joy they were disbelieving and still wondering." What do you think Jesus said next? Seemingly completely unfazed by all of this, Jesus asked them, "Have you anything here to eat?" (Luke 24:41). The disciples are completely baffled by this surprising encounter with Jesus. There is joy. There is disbelief. There is wonder. There is fear. There are questions. Yet, what Jesus seems most concerned about is, "Where's the beef?"

Most Christians have a hard time imagining Jesus as someone who would ask such a question. We imagine that our Lord and Savior spent all his time giving serious sermons, casting out demons, and engaging in deep and silent prayer. Yes, Jesus must have been serious because he was engaged in such serious business. He was saving the world after all! Yet, Jesus really enjoyed feasting. Time and time again, throughout the gospels we find Jesus sitting down at someone's house to eat, going to wedding parties, and telling parables about eating.

For example, consider the three parables of "lostness" in Luke 15. In the first, a shepherd leaves ninety-nine sheep in the wilderness to go and search for one that is lost. When he finds it, he "lays it on his shoulder and rejoices. And when he comes home, he calls together his friends and neighbors saying 'Rejoice with me, for I have found my sheep that was lost'" (Luke 15:5–6). The same is true of the woman who in the next parable loses a single coin. She lights a lamp and sweeps the house until she finds it. And when she does she calls together her friends and neighbors saying, "Rejoice with me, for I have found the coin that I had lost" (Luke 15:9). However, these two celebrations pale in comparison with the one given by a father whose son "was dead and is [now] alive; he was lost and is found" (Luke 15:24). Even the best robe, a ring for his finger, sandals on his feet, and killing the fatted calf cannot quite contain the joy and celebration.

As opposed to being a killjoy, Jesus' eating and drinking is such a major component of his ministry that he is accused of being a glutton and a drunk: "For John the Baptist has come eating no bread and drinking no wine, and you say 'He has a demon'; the Son of Man has come eating and drinking and you say, 'Look, a

glutton and a drunkard, a friend of tax collectors and sinners!'"
(Luke 7:33–34). My point is not that Christians should overindulge
themselves with dessert and wine. In our American culture of abundance, many fall prey to the sin of gluttony far too often. However,
following Jesus does mean feasting and knowing joy through table
fellowship, even in the face of serious religious folks who frown on
frivolity.

Where's the Feast?

Jesus enjoyed the feast. We love to eat. And there is a difference.
To feast is to participate in a wonderful gift. To eat is to fill our
bodies with calories. In many ways, because it is so easy to eat in
abundance, Christians seem to have lost their ability to "feast." Professor L. Shannon Jung writes: "Feasting has fallen into disrepute.
In a religion suffused with the reality of resurrection, liberation,
deliverance, grace, and celebration, one might expect feasting to
be a central practice. And it used to be. For us, however, feasting
tends to connote more of what we already have too much of—food
piled on top of more food. Our problem is too much rather than
too little."[2]

Yes, in the United States we have available to us an overabun-
dance of food. When I was young, my grandfather's cousin Franz
came to visit with us for a week or so. At the time, Franz lived in
communist controlled East Germany. He spoke very little English,
so my grandfather translated as we talked with one another. One
evening my father asked Franz what most surprised him about
America. Without hesitation, Franz replied through my grandfather, "the grocery store." The amount of food in American grocery
stores completely overwhelmed him. Instead of single brand of
cereal, there was a whole aisle of choices. Instead of a few bananas
available once a month, there were hundreds every day. Franz could
not comprehend the size and the scope and the quantity of food
available.

2. Jung, *Sharing Food*, 57.

Now one would think that in the face of such abundance, our first response would be gratitude. Thanks be to God for such wonderful gifts. However, for the last three hundred years or so we are conditioned in our Western culture to think that if we hope to experience this material abundance we will have to either create it or take it.[3] Our culture today leads us to believe that we get what we deserve and that we can expect to succeed if there is a level playing field. We teach our children what we learned from our parents and grandparents—always do your best because hard work guarantees success. We strive to climb the corporate ladder so as to take new jobs that come with greater responsibility and more lucrative pay. As we age, we see our elders loathing the need to rely on the kindness of family and friends because, "I can take care of myself."

Self-reliance has always been an American virtue, but it is not a Christian virtue. Caring for oneself and others in the community is a wonderful response to God's grace. However, the problem emerges when we actually believe that everything depends upon us. Because if everything good in my life is due to my skill, hard work, and achievement, then gratitude becomes unnecessary. When Christians adopt this attitude, is it any wonder that their celebration of the Lord's Supper, which my Presbyterian liturgy calls, "the joyful feast of the people of God,"[4] turns into something that resembles a funeral for Jesus? The elders wear dark clothes, the organist plays slow, sorrowful music, and no one speaks above a whisper. These Christians do not expect to joyfully encounter our resurrected Lord at this table. No, they all lift small glasses as if in a toast to a departed host.

Thank You God for Giving Us Food!

After our church's Wednesday night dinner, I typically lead a Bible study for adults. Meanwhile, the children of the church participate in music and education programs. Over the course of a month, the children rotate into different workshops so they might experience a Bible

3. See Alain De Botton, *Status Anxiety*, "Meritocracy."

4. Book of Common Worship, "Invitation to the Lord's Table," 68.

story or Christian practice in several unique ways. It is a wonderful program and well attended by preschool and elementary-age children.

This past spring the children engaged in a monthlong study of prayer. My Christian education colleague asked if I would be willing to teach the children one Wednesday night about bedtime prayers and table grace. She even offered to lead my adult Bible study so I could spend that time with the kids! Even if she hadn't extended me this offer to trade responsibilities, I would have said yes.

Three groups of children came to my workshop that night. Each workshop lasted for about twenty minutes. Knowing I did not have a lot of time with them, I prepared a brief lesson on bedtime prayers, and then a quick craft that included a cardstock tea cup. The idea was that this cup could be placed on the dinner table at home as a reminder for them to pray before eating. However, we spent most of the workshop learning to sing various table graces. We sang the Johnny Appleseed grace; we belted out "God is Great" to the tune of Final Jeopardy; and we even learned a prayer of thanksgiving to the musical theme of Spiderman. But the favorite of all was the Superman Grace. It goes like this (if you are alone you can try it with the motions if you like):

> *(Stand with your feet slightly apart and your hands on your hips.)*
> "Thank you God for giving us food!"
> *(As you say this line extend your right hand above your head.)*
> "Thank you God for giving us food!"
> *(Extend your left hand above your head.)*
> "Our daily bread, we must be fed!"
> *(Pretend you are flying like Superman.)*
> "Thank you God for giving us food!"
> *(Right hand extended, left hand on your hip.)*
> "Amen." (*Both hands on your hips.*)

The kids at church loved it. For weeks, every time they saw me they would laugh; throw a hand in the air, and say, "Thank you God for giving us food!" Months later, parents still told me stories of their child asking to say the Superman Grace before dinner.

What would be it like if we came to the Lord's Table not as if we were preparing for a funeral, but with the excitement and energy of the Superman Grace? Could it truly be an experience of thanksgiving? Could we expect to encounter Jesus at his table? Could we cease our endless striving and accomplishment and actually receive the feast as a gift of grace?

Not the Last Supper

Joy came to the whole world through the cross, but as Alexander Schmemann has written, "We have no other means of entering into joy, no way of understanding it, except through the one action which from the beginning has been for the church both the source and the fulfillment of joy, the very sacrament of joy, the Eucharist."[5] The Greek word we translate as "Eucharist," *eucharisto,* means "thanksgiving." As writer Ann Voskamp points out in her moving book on joy, *One Thousand Gifts,* the word *eucharisto* contains the Greek word for joy, *chara.*[6] While I disagree with Voskamp that the extent to which we experience joy is dependent upon the depths of our thanksgiving, I do think that gratitude is one of the ways we might meet Christ in a culture that says everything depends upon us and that we deserve everything we get. As we give thanks, particularly as we give thanks around a table where Christ has promised to meet us, we might see him and know joy.

Let us recall that it was as Jesus' earthly ministry drew to a close, he shared a final meal with his disciples. They shared not an ordinary meal; it was the Passover meal: a meal of celebration and liberation, a meal of remembrance and hope based on God's formative act of deliverance from slavery. It was a meal of joy. While we hear "Last Supper" and we think of death, Passover is a meal of great joy. Even though his death was coming, Jesus and the disciples shared a feast to remember and celebrate God's gracious saving acts both in history and today, salvation that was to be enacted once and for all in the cross and resurrection of Jesus himself.

5. Schmemann, *For theLife*, 25.
6. Voskamp, *One Thousand Gifts*, 33.

This same sense of grace-filled and joyful eating continues three days later, as we've already seen in the Gospel of Luke's resurrection day account of meals in Emmaus and Jerusalem. Turns out that Passover was not the "last" supper after all!

Even more feasting occurs after Easter evening. In the Gospel of John, seven of the disciples return to Galilee and decide to go fishing on the sea (John 21:1–14). Recall that Jesus meets them on the shore and, in a scene straight from a late-night comedy show, Peter puts on his clothes and jumps into the sea to swim to Jesus. By the time Peter gets to the shore and the other disciples arrive with a boatload of fish, Jesus has started a charcoal fire. He then cooks them breakfast. None of the disciples dared to ask him who he was because they knew that it was the Lord. Just as it happened during his earthly life, so it happened during his resurrection appearances: when Jesus' disciples eat together, Jesus is present with them and they recognize him.

And so it can be for us. To come to the Lord's Table as disciples today should not be to attend a funeral for Jesus. No, to come to this table is to be present at a resurrection feast, just like in Emmaus, Jerusalem, and by the Sea of Galilee so many years ago. Jesus has promised to show up at his table of thanksgiving. When we recognize him there we will know joy.

Babette's Feast

But even more than that, such an experience of thanksgiving, a recognition of the power of grace in our lives as we gather to feast, draws us into community. Although we can eat alone, we cannot feast all by ourselves. To experience the feast is to experience joy. As the poet W. H. Auden has written, "In a state of panic, a man runs round in circles by himself. In a state of joy, he links hands with others and they dance round in a circle together."[7] Yes, to feast together is to know joy.

When I was in seminary, my worship class professor invited the class to his house to watch a movie called *Babette's Feast*. I did

7. Auden, "Hic et Ill," 100.

not know it at the time, but the film won the 1987 Academy Award for Best Foreign Language film. The movie, set in nineteenth-century Denmark, is about two adult unmarried sisters who live in an isolated village with their father, the honored and beloved pastor of a small Protestant church. After their father's death, the sisters continue to carry on his legacy, which includes a quite severe and ascetic lifestyle.

Soon a French refugee named Babette arrives at the sisters' door and begs them to take her in as a maid, housekeeper, and cook. For the next fourteen years, Babette modestly and simply works for the sisters and gradually becomes part of their lives and the lives of many in the village. Babette's only link to her former life in Paris is a lottery ticket, which a friend renews for her every year. As luck would have it, one year she wins 10,000 francs. With her winnings, Babette offers to prepare a delicious dinner for the sisters and small congregation on the occasion of the pastor's hundredth birthday. Having no idea how much such a feast would cost, the sisters agree.

Babette goes to Paris to buy the ingredients. When she returns, the sisters and various members of the congregation grow concerned that the feast will be too lavish and even potentially sinful. So as not to offend Babette, in a hasty conference the sisters and the congregation agree to eat the meal, but to not take pleasure in it or speak about the food during the entire dinner.

When it is time to eat, everyone sits quietly at the table. Each course appears and is more delicious and exquisitely prepared than the one before. One visitor joins the party but is not privy to the agreement to refrain from commenting on the food. He lavishes praise on each dish, comparing the feast to a meal he enjoyed in Paris many years ago.

As the meal progresses, as each dish is sampled, as the wine with each course is poured, the dour and somber faces of the sisters and members of the congregation begin to soften. Eventually a smile is exchanged and a few words of kindness. Laughter erupts and Babette is called forth from the kitchen for a word of thanks and congratulations. The sisters assume that after the feast and with her lottery winnings, Babette will return to Paris and her former life. However, Babette tells the sisters that she is not going anywhere. She had been a famous chef in Paris before she became a refugee, but this meal was an act of thanksgiving, a gift to the sisters and community for their hospitality and care for her in her time of need. Her winnings are gone as she had spent every franc on the feast.

The guests are astonished at this act of gratitude. They are transformed by it. The meal concludes with dessert and a final drink, and the guests begin to depart. As they make their way outside, the moon shines brightly in the sky above the small village square. One of the congregation members begins singing a song of thanksgiving and praise. The others slowly join him. Someone offers a hand to another and soon, "in a state of joy" they link hands and dance in circles together. The feast was a gift. It allowed the participants to know the joy of thanksgiving, the joy of a community singing and dancing together.

Rip and Dip

At the church I serve, we have two worship services each Sunday. Our early morning service is a unique blend of worship styles. The music is led by guitars and vocalists. Many, although not all, of the songs we sing are songs you might hear on a contemporary Christian radio station. And, perhaps most important, we celebrate the Lord's Supper every week at the early morning service. The second service is more traditional in terms of its worship styles and music, and it does not feature a weekly celebration of the Lord's Supper. However, I preach the same sermon at the early morning service as I do at the later, more traditional service.

Some have suggested that the risk of weekly communion is that the sacrament can become rote and lose its meaning. If we allow the Lord's Table to turn into a funeral for Jesus, then I agree it would be dreadful to celebrate communion every Sunday.

However, my experiences during the early morning service have provided me an insight into the celebratory nature of the Lord's Supper. Each week during this early morning service I find myself in a different place in my life, and my faith, when I approach the table. Some weeks I need Christ to nourish and strengthen me with the bread and juice. Other weeks I celebrate with thanksgiving the gifts that I or others have received. Often I find myself joining the line to the table feeling connected to my brothers and sisters in Christ in ways I only find here.

Yet, the trips to the table in which I have best encountered Christ, and known joy over the last several years, are the ones I have taken with my daughter Bekah. Bekah is the youngest. She is our only girl. It might be fair to say that she has her daddy wrapped around her finger. Several years ago on a Sunday when Sarah and the kids worshipped at the early service, as I stepped away from the table after inviting the congregation to come forward for the bread and cup, Bekah made her way out of the row where she was sitting, came up to me, and put her arms in the air so I would pick her up. This service is a relaxed service, so I did exactly as she asked.

After inviting the congregation to come forward I usually walk to the back of the room so as to be the final one to receive communion. On this particular day I carried Bekah with me. The Praise Team began to play and the congregation began to sing as each row made its way to the front of the room. Two elders, who never wear black suits, stood in front of the table. One held the loaf of bread and the other a chalice filled with grape juice. When a congregation member reached the front of the line, he or she broke off a small piece of bread and dipped it in the cup. The formal name for celebrating communion in this way is "intinction." However, when we were kids, we always called it "Rip and Dip"!

That particular morning I joined the line at the end. Singing as we went, I made my way forward while carrying Bekah in my arms. While not all churches follow this practice, our church does not have a minimum age for receiving communion. The table is open to all who are invited by Christ to come. And, as Christ said, "Let the little children come to me." So when I reached the elder holding the bread, I broke off a small piece. Bekah reached out her small hand and took a whole fist full of bread. Nearly a quarter of the remaining loaf now sat firmly in her hand! Her eyes grew wide and her face broke into the biggest grin! I had to laugh. She had a hard time fitting her bread into the chalice, but finally it emerged dripping with grape juice. She took a bite, jumped out of my arms, and ran back to her seat to show her mother what she had done.

And Christ, definitely present there, smiled and I knew the gift of joy. Every Sunday since, when she is at the early morning service, Bekah has come running to me. Until the last few months I have picked her up. But she has grown, so now we join hands, walk side by side, and joyfully rip and dip together.

Questions for Reflection

1. Describe the experience of celebrating the Lord's Supper at your church? Is it the joyful feast of the people of God? Why or why not?

2. Do you have trouble imagining Jesus as someone who enjoyed feasting? If so, why do you think that image is hard for you?

3. It is often hard in my family's busy schedule to sit down together for dinner and to say grace. What is your family's experience of eating dinner together, and what kinds of prayers do you use to say thanks?

4. How do you struggle against the expectation that everything depends upon you, and you should get only what you deserve? Does your church or faith community help you with this struggle?

5. How would you talk about the connection between thanksgiving and joy? Have you known joy through moments of gratitude?

8

A Week from Next Tuesday

1 Peter 1:3-9 and Revelation 22:16-21

NOW THAT YOU HAVE made it to the last chapter of this book, for which I am extremely grateful, I have a confession to make. When I myself read a book, especially a novel, I have been known to succumb to a certain temptation from time to time. When I read a well-written, deliberate work of fiction, I try my best to stand strong and resist it. The temptation hits me much harder when reading a mystery or a detective novel. But no matter what I read, even when I used to read *Goodnight Moon* to my children before bedtime, the temptation was always there. And the temptation is this: to read the end of the book before it is time.

The urge to flip to the last page doesn't usually hit me until I am about a third of the way into a book. The plot has grown interesting, but the hour is late. I know it is not long before I need to turn off the light and go to sleep. The temptation comes. I will just read the last sentence, I tell myself—or just the last paragraph, or maybe just the last page. Usually I can keep it at that, no more than the last page, but from that moment on I fight a constant struggle to not read the end of the book before it is time.

Perhaps you also struggle with this temptation. Do you succumb to this longing in the midst of reading a good story? Surely you did not turn to the end of this book before it was time! Do not feel bad if you did—I wrote the epilogue long before much of the rest. Anyway, I suspect that either in this book, or in another, you have flipped to the last page to see how the book will end. It is a natural inclination for most of us. We want to know what the future holds. Even in the fictional world of a novel we want to know how the conflicts or challenges or issues will be resolved. And how much more so is this the case in our own lives?

Throughout this book I have used the phrase "a week from next Tuesday" to talk about some unknown day in the future. We never know what a week from next Tuesday is going to hold. It may be an ordinary day filled with quite regular activities and demands. Most of the time that is exactly what a week from next Tuesday will hold.

However, a week from next Tuesday may be a most unexpected day. Just two weeks ago, as I prepared breakfast for the kids, an unbearable shooting pain suddenly gripped my back and right side. I reached the bedroom, took off my shirt and tie, and collapsed on the bed. In twenty minutes I was supposed to lead a men's Bible study, but I literally could not stand, nor could I sit or lie still. I called my doctor, who attends the Bible study, to say that I was not going to be there. He said to come to his office that very morning. I had no idea what was wrong. It turns out that the worst pain of my life was the result of a kidney stone less than three millimeters in size. It caught me completely off guard. As I have learned, it is impossible to know what a week from next Tuesday will hold.

Sometimes we want to know the future, what a week from next Tuesday holds, so that we might live differently in the present. I know I drink a lot more water now that I know my future might hold another kidney stone. And yet, so often, we seek to know the future so that we can shape it and control it. It is so easy to take God's amazing blessings and turn them into goals that we ourselves can achieve with a little bit of hard work. If we are honest, most of us have bought into our culture of achievement. We have goals for our personal lives, for our communities, and for our churches. We have dreams for our children, our jobs, our retirement, and our ministry together. We have plans for tomorrow, and next week, and next month, and next year. And yet very few, if any, of those goals, dreams, and plans are such that we cannot accomplish them on our own with a little luck and a lot of hard work. And when we do, we say, "Wow, look what I have done. God sure must be proud of me."

However, no matter how diligently we plan and we vision and we set goals and we worry, ultimately we cannot control a week from next Tuesday. If we allow ourselves a moment of honesty, we have no idea if our best laid plans will be dashed on the rocks of unexpected illness or tragedy or stock market crash. We cannot control whether all our work, our hopes, and our dreams will grow and flourish even beyond our wildest expectations. A week from next Tuesday may be quite ordinary or it may be filled with the unexpected. Ultimately the future does not rest in our hands and, if we are willing to admit it, that scares us more than a little.

So, how often do we wish that we could flip to the end of the book? How often do we long to read the last sentence, the last paragraph, or even the last page and see how all will turn out? More precisely, how strongly do we wish for this ability when we are looking for joy?

The Intersection of Memory and Hope

Whenever I mention to someone that I am working on a project related to joy and how Christians might know joy, the other person always at least seems interested. As they ask me more and as I try to explain, their curiosity rarely fades. Almost universally, it seems, we possess a longing to know true joy. In the introduction to this book I called the search for joy as a longing for "something more."

Author C. S. Lewis describes joy as a particular kind of longing. In his early years, Lewis was awakened to a kind of joy through the music of the German composer Wagner, and then through the tales of Norse and Celtic mythology. Yet as he listened to more music, as he read more myths, he realized that while he had accumulated intellectual knowledge, he had lost the excitement and joy the music and myths once evoked. Even more, all his attempts to recover the old thrill proved fruitless.

But then, when he felt all hope was lost, there arose "the memory of a place and time at which [he] had tasted the lost Joy with unusual fullness." He writes about remembering that experience:

> It had been a particular hill walk on a morning of white mist. The other volumes of the [myths I had been reading] had just arrived as a Christmas present from my father, and the thought of all the reading before me, mixed with the coldness and loneliness of the hillside, the drops of moisture on every branch, and the distant murmur of the concealed town, had produced a longing (yet it was also fruition) which had flowed over from the mind and seemed to involve the whole body. That walk I now remembered . . . If only such a moment could return! But what I realized was that it had returned—that the remembering of that walk was itself a new experience of just the same kind. True, it was desire, not possession. But then what I had felt on that walk had also been desire.[1]

Lewis knew joy not through possession of it, but as he remembered the "longing and yet also fruition" that had so captured him on that hillside walk. To remember that moment and to long for it again had somehow, surprisingly, made joy present.

We find this same connection of recollection and longing in the first chapter of 1 Peter. First Peter is addressed to the small number of Christians living throughout the Roman provinces in Asia Minor. Most of these Christians had converted to the faith from Gentile and pagan backgrounds. Thus, they lived in tension not only with their fellow citizens but also with their families and friends who regarded their conversion as suspect. Sounds a lot like the experience of many Christians today!

Recognizing the challenges of living in the midst of tension with their culture, Peter begins his letter with thanksgiving to God for new life through the resurrection of Jesus Christ. Thus, he remembers and celebrates liberation from sin and death. Remembering God's gracious act in Jesus Christ also allows him to remind his readers of the gift of an "imperishable, undefiled, and unfading inheritance" to be "revealed in the last time" (1 Pet 1:3). Even in

1. Lewis, *Surprised by Joy*, 166.

a time of persecution, hostility, and "various trials" for these new Christians, this memory allows them to know "a new birth into a living hope." The present is lived where this memory of liberation meets this living hope for an eternal inheritance.

If that seems a little heady, try thinking about the connection between memory and hope in this way. Imagine that you, with all the knowledge of today that you possess, are suddenly transported to your hometown one hundred years in the future. Undoubtedly the world will look differently because time has passed. Perhaps the church that you love has fallen on hard times. Membership, mission, and giving have all declined. It has been so long since the church felt alive that despair fills the few remaining members.

However, you arrive with the memory of a flourishing religious life and community. This memory gives you hope that the future can look differently than what you see in the declining church. You remember what the past was like, and you can tell the story of life lived differently. You stand at the intersection of memory and hope.

Just like the early Christians in Asia Minor to which Peter wrote, just like C. S. Lewis's recollection of a hillside walk, as people of faith we stand at the intersection of memory and hope. We remember and know God's mighty acts of deliverance through the life, death, and resurrection of Jesus Christ. Based on this "memory" we know that God is for us and will act for us in the future. Despite knowing times of trial in the present, we hope with anticipation for the fullness of life that is to come. Life is lived at that crossroads. And as memory crosses hope, what we are invited to know is joy. Peter writes: "Although you have not seen him, you love him; and even though you do not see him now, you believe in him and rejoice with an indescribable and glorious joy, for you are receiving the outcome of your faith, the salvation of your souls" (1 Pet 1:8–9).

Even in the moment when we cannot see Christ, we might still know joy. For to stand at the intersection of memory and hope, to know joy, is to cling with faith and longing to the acts of God for us in Jesus Christ. It is to "see" Christ with our memory. What God has done for us in the past we can expect God to do for us in the future. Thus, with assurance and hope, we may joyfully face every future because we know that each and every moment is held in the hands of the God who has already redeemed the world through a life, a death, and an empty tomb. In a messy world, let us always be mindful of this amazing gift.

Lookout for Gratitude

However, and as I have tried to illustrate throughout this book, it is hard to know, to sustain, the joy of that memorable moment. So often, instead of being liberated by our memory, we fall into the trap of trying to hold on to or re-create the past. And thus, like C. S. Lewis, we dig deeper and we learn more, but we lose the joy we once knew. Obligation, burden, and entitlement replace what were once joyful encounters with Christ. Think of those church or family traditions that were wonderful when they began, but now we do only because we have always done them. Shed light on these musty relics and you will reveal the traps laid by memory.

And yet, even if somehow we manage to remember rightly so that our memories serve as the foundation for new moments of liberation and joy, the pendulum often swings too far the other direction. Instead of anticipating with hope and expectation, instead of rejoicing that the promises of God in Jesus Christ are true and reliable, we fear the future. We worry about what might be, instead of trusting what we know will be. Fear and anxiety hinder us as we seek to secure a future for ourselves and those we love. We become busy and serious with demands that can never be met and, once again, our joy dissipates.

But the good news of the gospel is that God invites us to more than obligation and entitlement, to more than fear and worry. As we stand at the intersection of memory and hope, we may "rejoice with an indescribable and glorious joy." Despite our best efforts to squelch its presence, joy keeps showing up because Christ keeps showing up. As a gift, joy comes to us wherever memory meets hope. Thus, to live joyfully means to be awake, to be watching, so that when the gift comes, we might rejoice and give thanks. As Karl Barth writes, "To be joyful is to expect that life will reveal itself as a gift of God's grace . . . to be joyful means to look out for opportunities for gratitude."[2]

Thus, joy comes as a gift in a variety of times and circumstances. There is a story about two men who walked together down an inner-city street. They had grown up in this neighborhood, and each man remembered a very different place. Now, buildings were in disrepair; graffiti covered the walls, broken glass littered the sidewalk. The one man looked at the surroundings and despaired. He thought, "What a waste of good resources. These old buildings must be repainted, the windows must be repaired. But why bother? Someone will probably just deface and destroy them again."

The other man looked at the same walls full of graffiti and was grateful. Instead of vandalism he saw beauty, creativity, and art. He looked at the shards of glass on the sidewalk and noticed the sun filtering through them, producing thousands of rainbows. He thought, "If there can be such beauty and wonder here, then this neighborhood can be saved. Thanks be to God."

At the intersection of memory and hope, we are invited to know joy in Christ. We are invited to live with anticipation, with eager expectation, for God to reveal his goodness and grace at any moment. We are invited to look out for opportunities for gratitude, and so we keep looking, anticipating, expecting, and turning to the end of the book.

The End of the Book

Maybe at some point in your life you opened the Bible in hopes of finding the answer to all of life's questions. Maybe you started with Genesis and read through Exodus and got bogged down in Leviticus or Numbers. Or maybe someone told you to begin with the New Testament. You read through the gospels, Matthew, Mark, Luke, and John. While there, you fell in love with Jesus. Then you began to travel with the apostles in the Book of Acts as the good news spread throughout the world. However, perhaps Paul's arguments about grace and law wore you down in Romans or Galatians,

2. Barth, *Church Dogmatics*, 3/4: 378.

or his advice about church conflict and authority turned you off in First or Second Corinthians. But whether it was in the Old Testament or the New Testament, that urge hit you. You thought, "I wonder how all this will end?" So you flipped to the back of the book.

And there you found The Revelation of John—a strange letter to seven churches—the words of prophesy . . .

When I was in high school, the church in which I grew up wanted to purchase new pew Bibles for the sanctuary. About that time, in a catalog or in a magazine, I saw a great deal on new Bibles. It seems that the printer had printed a large run of Bibles that contained a single error: the last verse of the Book of Revelation had been omitted. They did not discover the error until the printing was complete, and so they attempted to sell these Bibles on the cheap. I told my pastor about this and said that we should get these Bibles for our church. My sales pitch: "It doesn't matter. No one is going to read to the end of Revelation anyway!"

My pastor responded that it mattered a great deal. Having all of the Scriptures in the Bible was of great importance. We would not be buying Bibles that lacked a verse, especially a verse from the Book of Revelation.

Revelation begins with a promise: "Blessed is the one who reads aloud the words of the prophecy and blessed are those who hear and keep what is written in it" (Rev 1:3). Because of this promise, we start to wonder about that blessing as we read through the book and its dramatic visions. Horrible plagues accompany the opening of seven seals, the blowing of seven trumpets, and the pouring out of the seven bowls. Great devastation surrounds the fall of Babylon—code for the Roman Empire. A lamb does battle with the dragon; a pregnant woman drops into the midst of a battle and is threatened by a dragon. The earth itself acts to rescue the woman with her child and the lamb fights with a sword that comes from the lamb's mouth—the word of God.

If we hold on to our courage and persistence, if we keep reading, we find another vision—this time of a city descending from a new heaven to take its place on a new earth. This city is a New Jerusalem where there will be no death, no more tears, and no night—for the home of God is with us! A crystal clear river flows from the throne of God. No longer is there anything to fear lurking beneath the waves of the sea—for the sea is no more!

If we manage to make our way through all those visions, if we succeed in not giving up and scratching our heads in bewilderment, then we are finally ready to read the end of the book. The last page. And in the end, Jesus Christ himself speaks for the first time in Revelation (Rev 22:16). Jesus seems to confirm all that has gone before. As Brian Blount, president of Union Presbyterian Seminary, writes: "All along, John's dramatic visions have had a single intent: to shock those who were operating against God and the Lamb into testifying to and for them, while encouraging those who were already testifying to stay the difficult course . . . John pictures the future in such a way that he hopes will either entice or frighten hearers and readers into making the appropriate decision to line up behind the lordship of God and the Lamb."[3]

So if you need to be scared into straightening up and flying right, Christ gives you one last warning that dogs and sorcerers and fornicators and murders and idolaters and everyone else who loves falsehood will be left outside of the new city. If you need encouragement to persevere, then Christ shares a vision of robes cleansed in blood and free access to the holy city and the tree of life. Whatever you need to make a decision about being a witness for Christ today—you can find it here, at the end of the book.

And so, as we at last reach the end of the Book of Revelation, the end of the Bible, it seems that the final verse does matter after all. We still want to know how the story will end, what the future holds. And, in that final verse, what we find is a promise. "The one who testifies to these things says, 'Surely I am coming soon.' Amen. Come, Lord Jesus! The grace of the Lord Jesus be with all. Amen" (Rev 22:20–21).[4]

I have suggested throughout this book that joy is a gift received each and every time we know Christ's presence with us. I am convinced that Christ's promise at the end of the Book of Revelation doesn't just apply to Christ's "second coming" at the end of

3. Blount, *Revelation*, 405–6.
4. Ibid., 416–17.

history. No, Christ promises to be with us always, and surely he is coming soon.

In the midst of our busyness we look for joy and we want to know how the story will end. Jesus promises, "Surely I am coming soon." In surprising and unexpected ways today and a week from next Tuesday, in our busy and ordinary lives, he does.

In the midst of personal tragedy, pain, and even death we look for joy and we want to know how the story will end. Jesus promises, "Surely I am coming soon." Through the cross and an empty tomb today and a week from next Tuesday, with assurance and hope, he does.

In the midst of our struggles to create all good things for ourselves we look for joy so that we can be sure of how the story ends. Jesus promises, "Surely I am coming soon." With thanksgiving in hands joined, as memory crosses hope today and a week from next Tuesday, he does.

So we respond with blessing and praise. "The grace of the Lord Jesus be with all. Amen." Could it really be anything else but grace? All the dramatic visions in that book ultimately lead to grace—not just for some, but for all.

That is how the story ends. These words of prophecy are not sealed. They are open, so you can read that final verse anytime you want. A flip to the final page is to find a gift, a promise, a blessing for you and for me. "Surely I am coming soon . . . The grace of the Lord Jesus be with all."

Come, Lord Jesus!

As I hope you come to see throughout this book, the quest to know joy and see Christ's presence is a very personal one for me. It has not always been an easy journey. Several years ago, when I finished the first draft of my doctor of ministry thesis, I wrote this:

> As a young adult myself who is well aware of the demands and pressures of work, family, and especially church, this project has been a personal quest for me. I sought to discover whether I could make a commitment

to these Sabbath practices in my own life, and if doing so would promote my own openness to and greater knowledge of joy in Christ. I regret to report that in some ways the project has had the exact opposite effect. Instead of spending time doing as little or as much as the day brings, what had previously been my Sabbath time became filled with crafting Bible studies and keynote presentations! I confess I often thought that if there was anything good or joyful to be found in this project, it depended upon me to create it. Lack of sleep due to sitting at the computer long after my wife and children had gone to bed led to more than a handful of days filled with despair.

So I come to the end, perhaps having led others to a greater knowledge of joy in Christ while at the same time diminishing my own. Joy remains as elusive as ever. But, even in this there is hope. For if joy could be created or measurably increased through my leading of this or any other project, then joy would not be the gift I have claimed it to be. Christ says, "So you have pain now; but I will see you again, and your hearts will rejoice and no one will take your joy from you" (John 16:22).

So I pray, "Come, Lord Jesus!"

That was the end, the final page, the final sentence in the draft of my thesis that I turned into my advisors and a few friends. I wrote the final sentence at the end of a very long and solitary week of writing sixteen hours a day in a small room on a seminary campus in Richmond, Virginia. In truth I not only wrote that sentence, I prayed it.

And as I opened my heart to God in that moment, Christ came. And so did joy.

I knew joy in that moment, not because the thesis was finished but because Christ was there and I palpably perceived his presence.

Everyone who read the initial draft of my thesis commented on the end. Some worried about me, while others wondered at my candor. Many recognized, as I did, that my emotional and spiritual struggles over the course of the project and writing of the thesis acutely exemplified the essence of the project itself. Not wanting to deny the despair I felt at that moment and yet needing to celebrate my joy in Christ, I left the final sentence exactly as I had written it, but I also added an epilogue.

In the years since I completed that initial draft of my thesis, I have continued to know the joy that accompanied my prayer. My life is a daily journey of looking for Christ, catching a glimpse of him in the midst of my busyness, the tragedy around me, and my own quest for control. In those rare moments of clarity, I receive a wondrous gift. In these pages I have tried to give you a glimpse of that amazing gift so that you might begin to see joy in your own life.

However, as we reach the end of this book, please remember that there is a lifetime of practice needed before we might see Christ face to face and know as we have been truly known (1 Cor 13:12). The more we strive for joy, the less of a gift of grace it becomes. Thus, with one eye squinted, I invite you to pray, "Come, Lord Jesus!" and to "Rejoice in the Lord always! Again, I say rejoice!"

Questions for Reflection

1. What do you imagine or hope that your life will be like five years from now? What goals have you set to ensure your life will turn out exactly as you think it should? Have you ever had to set a goal aside in order to follow Jesus?

2. In what ways do your memories influence how you live your life in the present? Have you ever experienced a time when "memory crossed hope" and you knew joy?

3. How often do you look for opportunities for gratitude? What would be different in your life if you lived with the expectation that every moment would reveal itself as a gift of God's grace?

4. What do you think of the Revelation to John? Have you ever read all the way to the end? Did you think Revelation might be an opportunity to see Christ and know joy?

5. What have you discovered about joy now that you have reached the end of the book?

6. What is your prayer as you think about your life a week from next Tuesday?

Epilogue

The Lord is Near

(A Sermon)

I PREACHED THIS SERMON at First Presbyterian Church, Lumberton, in December 2009. These words were penned in the midst of one of the more difficult weeks I have known in ministry. I spent many hours on my knees in prayer listening for God's guidance in a situation that affected many. In the midst of challenging circumstances that did not lend themselves to happiness or pleasure, God blessed me with Philippians 4:4–7 as the epistle text suggested for that Sunday. I hope the following sermon captures much of what I have tried to share with you in the preceding pages of this book. For when Christ shows up and we know joy, do we have any choice but to proclaim the good news?

Rejoice in the Lord always; again I will say, Rejoice. Let your gentleness be known to everyone. The Lord is near. Do not worry about anything, but in everything by prayer and supplication with thanksgiving let your requests be made known to God. And the peace of God, which surpasses all understanding, will guard your hearts and your minds in Christ Jesus (Phil 4:4–7).

Several years ago I attended a conference where the keynote speaker told a story about his little girl. It seems that his daughter was preparing to enter kindergarten and in the state where they lived, each entering kindergartener was given a standardized test to assess his or her readiness to begin school. So, on the appointed day, her parents took their daughter to the school. A kind teacher met the little girl, walked her over to a desk, and sat down beside her. The teacher then asked mom and dad to wait outside the room and close the door. She said this would ease the pressure on their daughter, but talk about raising the anxiety of the parents!

Well, it wasn't long until the teacher came out of the room. Their daughter was still sitting at the desk coloring a picture. The teacher had a big smile on her face, but also a tear in her eye. She told the parents, "I asked your daughter a series of standard questions to which there are standard answers. For example, 'If I ask you to look at the sky, which way would you look?' The answer is 'up.' Well, I want you to know that your daughter has done very well and she is well prepared to begin kindergarten. But I also want to share with you the answer she gave to one of the questions. I asked your daughter, 'If you are going into a room that is dark what should you do?' The only acceptable answer according to the test is 'turn on the light.' However, your daughter said, 'If I was going into a room that is dark I would hold hands.' I can't give her credit for a correct answer, but I think it is the truest answer I've ever heard."

And so it is. If we are going into the darkness, we should reach out and hold someone's hand.

As we are moving through this season of Advent, we have talked about the accumulation of light. How each Sunday, as we move closer to Christmas, we light more candles on the Advent wreath to bear witness to the coming of light into the world. Well, today, on the third Sunday of Advent we have reached the third candle. You probably noticed that today we lit the only pink or rose colored candle. Often this candle is called the Joy candle. Its color represents the idea that today we take a break from the hard preparations of Advent. We sing a few joyful Christmas carols instead of the sometimes depressing Advent hymns. It is the day most often chosen for choir cantatas and musicals—just as we have done at the 11:00 service today.

And yet, even on this Sunday of joy, we can't seem to shake the idea that the darkness crouches just beyond the light of our three candles. And in less than thirty minutes when this worship service is over and those candles are extinguished, we're going to head back out into the darkness again.

Now, some of you simply know the darkness that manifests itself as general anxiety in a consumer culture. Others of you know the darkness that comes from a future that appears uncertain. Some of you know the darkness of illness, pain, anticipated surgery, treatment that seems worse than the disease, or a recovery taking longer than anticipated. Others of you know the darkness of loneliness and the prospect of another, or a first, Christmas without one you deeply loved. Some of you know the darkness of loved ones or friends at war, the darkness of violence much closer to home, or the darkness of fear. Perhaps the darkness waiting for you is known only by you. But we come to this place, to bask in the light, to escape the darkness, at least for a little while.

So it is with more than a little skepticism that we hear Paul's words to the Philippians in our text for today. "Rejoice in the Lord always. Again I say rejoice!" Rejoice—sometimes seems appropriate, doesn't it. Yes, joy might be just fine as a theme for worship today, when we can escape the darkness, even for a few moments. Joy might be just fine in these moments of blessed forgetfulness. But it is too much to ask for joy always, especially when we must walk back into the darkness once this service concludes.

My friends, there is a danger to thinking like that; to thinking that joy is only for the privileged and the few. To thinking that joy is only present in moments of escape and bliss and ease. And that danger is a temptation the early church called "Gnosticism." But we really don't need a fancy theological word for it, because it is the temptation to separate God from the world; the temptation to believe that salvation requires escape from the earthly, material things that imprison us. There is an attraction to wanting to escape the darkness, but to completely escape the darkness one must also leave behind the limits and challenges of things where that darkness resides. We must leave behind things like friendships, marriage, family, neighborhoods, congregations, and communities. As my friend Tom Currie of Union Presbyterian Seminary at Charlotte has written, trying to escape the darkness leads only to "loneliness."[1]

1. Currie, *Joy of Ministry*, 53.

For the one who tries to escape from the world finds that there is no one with whom to hold hands when the darkness returns.

Theologian Marva Dawn tells the story of the English actor Alec Guinness, perhaps best known as Obi Wan Kenobi from the original *Star Wars* movies, and how he began a journey from loneliness to faith.[2] It happened when Guinness was involved in a film playing the role of a priest. One dark night after a long day of filming, he walked back to the village where the actors were staying. Still dressed in his priestly garb he was joined on the road by a frightened little boy. The boy reached out and took Guinness's hand, trustingly clinging to it all the way to the village. Faced with the darkness, the boy reached out to hold hands. Guinness began at that point to wonder, if this small stranger could trust a "man of God," whether the God of the church must be trustworthy also.

And so he is. Trustworthy to his promises not to leave us alone, to be with us always, to come not as an angel, not as a spirit, not as a dream, but a child of flesh and blood right in the middle of all this darkness.

That is why Paul urges the Philippians to rejoice always. Not because of their circumstances or their happiness or their pleasure or their ability to escape from the darkness. No, Paul urges the Philippians to rejoice *in the Lord* always because "the Lord is near."

God knows that the darkness threatens to overwhelm us and so he draws near. To an unwed mother, in the midst of a stable full of animals, and into a world that didn't need another king, God comes to bring a little light, light that the darkness cannot overcome.

God comes down from the heavens; God draws close, so that when we reach out as the darkness closes in, the hand waiting to firmly and securely grasp our hand is God's.

So as this service today comes to a close, as we extinguish the Joy candle on the Advent wreath, at least until next Sunday, as we walk through those doors to the darkness that waits and maybe even threatens, let us join hands with one another. For often the hand of God feels like the hand of our wife or husband, the hand of a child or a parent, the hand of a brother or sister in Christ.

---

2. Dawn, *Sense of the Call*, 252.

Bibliography

Auden, W. H. "Hic et Ill," In *The Dyer's Hand and Other Essays*. New York: Vintage International, 1999.

Barth, Karl. *Church Dogmatics III.4*. Edinburgh: T&T Clark International, 2004.

Blount, Brian K. *Revelation: A Commentary—The New Testament Library*. Louisville: Westminster/John Knox, 2009.

Buechner, Frederick. *The Magnificent Defeat*. New York: Seabury, 1966.

Calvin, John. *Institutes of the Christian Religion*. Edited by John T. McNeill. Philadelphia: The Westminster Press, 1960.

Copenhaver, Martin B. "Laughter at Easter," *Journal for Preachers*, volume XXX, no. 3 (Easter 2007) 15-18.

Currie, Thomas W., III. *The Joy of Ministry*. Louisville: Westminster John Knox, 2008.

Dawn, Marva. *The Sense of the Call: A Sabbath Way of Life for Those Who Serve God, the Church, and the World*. Grand Rapids, MI: William B. Eerdmans, 2006.

De Botton, Alain. *Status Anxiety*. London: Penguin, 2005.

Edwards, Jonathan. "Treatise Concerning Religious Affections." In *A Jonathan Edwards Reader*, ed. John E. Smith, et al., 137–71. New Haven, CT: Yale University Press, 1995.

Goodwin, Craig. *Year of Plenty*. Minneapolis, MN: Sparkhouse, 2011.

Jung, L. Shannon. *Sharing Food: Christian Practices for Enjoyment*. Minneapolis, MN: Fortress, 2006.

Lewis, C. S. *Surprised by Joy*. Orlando, FL: Harcourt, 1955.

"The Long Lead Story." *Studio 60 on the Sunset Strip*, Season 1, Episode 5. NBC television.

Moltmann, Jurgen. *Theology and Joy*. Bristol, England: SCM, 1973.

Muller, Wayne. *Sabbath: Finding Rest, Renewal, and Delight in our Busy Lives*. New York: Bantam Books, 2000.

O'Connor, Flannery. "To Elizabeth and Robert Lowell—17 March 1953." In *Letters of Flannery O'Connor: The Habit of Being*, selected and edited by Sally Fitzgerald, 57–58. New York: Farrar, Straus, and Giroux, 1979.

Presbyterian Church (USA). *Book of Common Worship*. Prepared by the Theology and Worship Ministry Unit for the Presbyterian Church USA and the Cumberland Presbyterian Church. Louisville, KY: Westminster John Knox, 1993.

Bibliography

Rush, Kristie. "Update #37." (May 6, 2012). No pages. Online: http://kristierush. blogspot.com/2012_05_01_archive.html.

Schmemann, Alexander. *For the Life of the World.* Crestwood, NY: St. Vladimir's Seminary Press, 1973.

———. *The Journals of Alexander Schmemann 1973–1983.* Translated by Juliana Schmemann. Crestwood, NY: St. Vladimir's Seminary Press, 2000.

Tina Fey American Express Commercial. Video. Retrieved October 28, 2012, from www.youtube.com/watch?v=I7m-iAX3POU.

Voskamp, Ann. *One Thousand Gifts.* Grand Rapids, MI: Zondervan, 2010.

"What is My 95?" (Dec. 9, 2010). No Pages. Online: http://sendingout. com/2010/12/09/what-is-my95/.

Where's the Beef?. Video. Retrieved October 28, 2012, from www.youtube.com/ watch?v=Ug75diEyiA0.

Wright, Tom. *John for Everyone, Part Two.* Louisville: Westminster John Knox, 2004.

Yen, Hope. "1 in 2 new graduates are jobless or underemployed." No pages. Online: http://news.yahoo.com/1-2-graduates-jobless-underemployed -140300522.html.

Appendix

As DESCRIBED IN CHAPTER 2 of this book, take a moment to fill out this chart with all the activities and demands that fill your time in an average week. You may have some large blocks of time spent in one activity or you might detail every hour of every day. Choose whatever is most helpful to you.

Appendix

	Sun.	Mon.	Tues.	Wed.	Thurs.	Fri.	Sat.
5 a.m.							
6 a.m.							
7 a.m.							
8 a.m.							
9 a.m.							
10 a.m.							
11 a.m.							
12 p.m.							
1 p.m.							
2 p.m.							
3 p.m.							
4 p.m.							
5 p.m.							
6 p.m.							
7 p.m.							
8 p.m.							
9 p.m.							
10 p.m.							
11 p.m.							
12 p.m.							
1 a.m.							
2 a.m.							
3 a.m.							
4 a.m.							

Once you have filled in the chart with how you spend your time during an average week, complete the following:

1. Place a box around each item you believe is essential. This is something that you must do.

2. Place a circle around each item you believe is not essential, but so important that you do not want to give it up.

3. What does this chart reveal about how you spend your time?